ENDORSEMENTS

Out of the storms of life come God's revelation work into our hearts. Juan Martinez illustrates in this book, Beyond the Yellow Brick Road, the beauty of God's work as we journey toward Him. How God works to renew our mind, our heart, and to give us courage in the storms of life. All of God's work is personal within our storms and combines to bring us into relationship with Him. This is a book for every person seeking God and looking for the road to meaning, purpose, and a life with God.

Tom Lane
Apostolic Sr Pastor
Gateway Church
Southlake, Texas

Beyond the yellow brick road is one jewel of wisdom you must add to the treasure box. Every opposition we face in life is just another opportunity to display to those around us that we have promises that can be trusted from a God who cares about every detail of our lives. Pastor Juan Martinez truly describes the heartbeat of the father and points everyone into the direction that heals and restores - Jesus Christ

Bryann Trejo
Kingdom Muzic overseer minister of music

A few years ago, Pastor Juan Martinez entered my life much like he enters a room, as a whirlwind of energy and excitement that immediately lifts the atmosphere. This book "Beyond the Yellow Brick Road" details the source of that energy as he shares with us how to take on life from a victorious perspective.

Pastor Juan's story is a tale of him being radically transformed by an encounter with God and his continued pursuit to become all that he was created to be. This book will shift your thinking and inspire you to love and live life without restraint enabling you to truly experience the abundant life.

I'm so thankful that he has taken the time to articulate this journey so that everyone who reads it may have a greater understanding of God's love and goodness no matter what is happening around them. This book will change your life!

Pastor Brad Carter
Calvary Church North Carolina

It was around 11pm on the patio of a local coffee shop, where Pastor Juan spoke a life changing word to me, that would alter the course of my life and ministry. It was one of the most difficult, yet critical seasons, where my vision began to blur, and strength began to weaken, when he reminded me of who I am, and what God has called me to do.

It was that talk that spurred the beginning of critical ministry in our community that helps drug addicts and alcoholics find Christ. Pastor Juan has an ability to help people find their calling, or realign them in their calling. No matter where you are on your walk with Christ, this book will propel your journey with God.

Pastor Rey Sandoval
Rise Church

Beyond the Yellow Brick Road is all about unlocking the promises of God for our life. Pastor Juan Martinez paints such a beautiful picture for us of the hope that God created for all of us before we were ever even formed in our mothers womb. He validated us and chose us even knowing all the mistakes we would make in our life. What an incredible thought.

When His mercy meets our mess, everything changes. Pastor, I love everything about this book. It got the fire inside me ignited. This book totally describes the heartbeat of the Father and points us all in a direction that heals, restores and makes all things new. It's time to be all that God created us to be.

#RealTalkKim

Pastor Juan Martinez has been given a unique gift to communicate deep truth in a practical way. His love for Christ and people come to life with great encouragement that even in the storms we can have peace because God had all power.

David Vestal
Gateway Church Network.

"Jesus tells us those who have been forgiven much, love much. With a divine love like Juan Martinez has for people, you have to understand there's a backstory that brought him to this place. Pastor Juan has lived the highs and lows of life and has come out broken and with a limp but as a man that you know has been with God.

His insights of a deep relational walk with God will help everybody young and old make the most of their journey and their story. I'm thankful for Pastor Juan taking the time to share these deep, accessible truths to help the Body of Christ walk in a deeper relationship with Jesus!"

Mike Rosas
UpRising Society and Chaplain of the Houston Rockets

In every generation there are those who are always exploring the edges! It's on the edge that transformation takes place. Their curiosity causes them to reach beyond the norms of everyday life and discover 'secrets' that become the tools for building a life to those who will dare to follow them.

In his book, Beyond The Yellow Brick Road, my friend Juan Martinez helps us discover those secrets. From a life that once was on the wrong path to one that's been marked by amazing transformation, Juan's insights and stories will challenge you to 'get wrapped up' in God's promises and possibilities over your life. You will never be the same! I recommend you start your journey through the pages of this incredible story.

Tony Miller
Bishop - Destiny Fellowship of Churches

I have experienced first hand how God can change anyone. What started as a friendship, then lead to Mentorship, and now a spiritual parent to me Pastor Juan has not only been with me through my whole journey but has helped pave my own Yellow Brick Road. Juan's passion for Christ not only oozes out of his body but countless souls have witnessed God's hand through his powerful ministry. Beyond the Yellow Brick Road will not only give you insight to Juan's unique revelations but most of all will expose you to the Love of Jesus Christ. His transparency and ability to share the gospel can relate to those struggling but will also give great hope that there is another way out. Enjoy!

Vinny DeLeon
Pastor - Get Wrapped Church
Owner- Vinny's Barbershop

Juan is a man with fruit to his account. He embodies the transforming and loving power of God. The moment you meet him you instantly connect with him through the way He so easily welcomes people in and makes them feel like family. His heart is filled with genuine humility and love for people. You can tell He has a profound relationship with Jesus through the way that He loves and treats others and the way He leads his life. Juan is an excellent communicator with a passion to develop leaders and is a man of great character and integrity. He brings joy and laughter everywhere he goes.

Caleb Ring
Pastor, River Clermont Church

BEYOND THE YELLOW BRICK ROAD

UNLOCKING THE PROMISES OF GOD

JUAN MARTINEZ

FOREWORD BY JOHN RAMIREZ

COPYRIGHT

© 2020 *Juan Martinez*

First Edition

Cover Design: Wicked SmartCover Designs

Editorial Team: Imogen Howsen & Linda Ingmanson

Publisher: Five Stones Press, Dallas, Texas / For quantity sales, textbooks, and orders by trade bookstores or wholesalers contact Five Stones Press at publish@fivestonespress.net

Five Stones Press is owned and operated by Five Stones Church, a nonprofit 501c3 religious organization. Press name and logo are trademarked. Contact publisher for use.

Pastor Juan Martinez website: https://juanmartinez.tv/

Printed in the United States of America

DEDICATION

I dedicate this book to every person who is in prison, both behind the walls and to those incarcerated by the walls they have created within themselves, that are longing to be free.
May this book give you the courage to face the storms of life with a new heart and mind as you journey through the pages of this book.
Thank you Lord for setting us free.

CONTENTS

FOREWORD

I've traveled the world, helping people find true freedom through deliverance. But studies show that 87% of Christians never actually become free. Although believers escaped the personal bondage of Egypt, they clung to spiritual bondage and rejected something they never truly experienced—Freedom.

When Juan Martinez asked me to write the foreword for this book, I was honored to do so. Juan is a gift to the body of Christ. He's the real deal who has allowed the Gospel of Jesus Christ to transform his life. He wants everyone to experience the same Love that transformed his life.

Beyond the Yellow Brick Road is a masterpiece that will set many people on the path to freedom. Juan's story is a witness to the power of God. As you take this journey, let the Holy Spirit guide you and reveal truth in your life. This book will captivate you, touch you, and heal you.

Beyond The Yellow Brick Road is a metaphor for the right road that God has paved before the foundations of the earth. We are called to that path, and this is where we'll find our purpose and destiny.

This book will bring spiritual fulfillment, and it will open your spiritual eyes. It will give you clarity in your spirit and revelation of who you really are in Christ Jesus. I praise God for the ministry of Juan Martinez.

Evangelist John Ramirez

INTRODUCTION
WE ALL FACE STORMS

There'd be no sleeping that night. My wife, Ruthy, and I sensed something big was going down, but even the eerie quiet of a watchful vigil failed to reveal the truth. The reality was, Houston, Texas, was sitting smack dab in the path of Hurricane Harvey, and there wasn't a thing in the world we could do about it.

Ruthy and I rode a roller coaster of emotions as the hurricane barreled through the Gulf of Mexico. My gut was knotted as the Weather Channel crowed, "The storm is coming, the storm is coming." Unsure of what to believe, I finally allowed myself to relax when the weather experts downgraded the monster event from a hurricane to a mere tropical storm. That would be nothing to deal with, and I kind of laughed at myself for getting so worked up.

I wouldn't laugh for long as moisture-heavy Harvey decided to squat over the third-largest city in America. The hurricane dumped sixty inches of rain over four days. Houston was drowning in muddy brown floodwaters that showed no sign of stopping. Regret for not being better prepared kept me on a razor's edge. Still not grasping the enormity of the situation, I spent that fateful day spying through our living room window as neighbors escaped with what few belongings they could carry while wading through thigh-high waters.

By 2 p.m. the next day, the bayou behind our apartment building was swollen with floodwater. Brackish water sloshed onto our patio, and I knew it was time to go. We hustled up some clothing, a photo album my mom had given me of my childhood pics, and yes, all of my shoes. I know what you're thinking: shoes? Don't judge me. I love shoes (LOL).

Okay, so with water waist-deep, we rushed to collect a few things ready to take to a family member's home. Once there, we knew our stuff would be safe on the second floor. The feeling of safety was short-lived as there came a banging on the door, and a loud voice screamed, "It's time to leave. Grab your stuff and go." It was time to flee for our lives. With the little power I had left in my cell, I started making calls for rescue.

Our family at Get Wrapped Church has a lot of talented people. Thank God one pastor also was skilled at maneuvering his boat through a residential neighborhood. Once we were scooped up, our journey to safety began an all-day adventure across Houston—first a boat, then a van, then another boat, and finally a truck that drove us to our church's building. The panicked sounds of people screaming for help overwhelmed us as we floated through flooded areas searching for dry land.

My knuckles were hot white as I fought to stop myself from leaping out of the boat to help them, but in reality, what could I do? Their homes were being destroyed before their very eyes, and just like us, they'd soon have no place to call home. Ruthy reassured me that there were ample rescue boats making treks back and forth to pick up as many of those folks as possible.

I tried to settle my breathing as we held on to each other. I was grieving over what would also become even greater losses in the days to follow. Would it ever stop raining?

With my face buried against my wife's shoulder, I began to laugh. Not at the human suffering that surrounded us, but at the thought of what was printed on the raincoat I was given as a gift from a radio station where I hosted a show. In big, bold letters, it read, NOAH'S ARK. How ironic and appropriate.

Those printed words would become more relevant in the days ahead as we witnessed God's protection and provisions. Get Wrapped Church would become a major relief distribution center over the next month as people from all over the United States came in clutch with food, water, and other essentials for the hurting people of Houston.

But on that day of rescue, my heart was still heavy with the burden of loss. In a moment of self-pity, I huffed, "Aw man. God, I'm going to lose everything."

"You are?" God's response was immediate and sobering. I knew what He meant because the Holy Spirit filled in the blanks. I was sorry for having said that in a moment of weakness, but at the very same time, God showed His mercy in lovingly correcting me.

I understood that no matter what we lost, He could rebuild and give it back. Even if all we ended up with were the clothes on our backs, and yes, even that NOAH'S ARK raincoat, we would still have everything as long as we had Him.

Speaking of clothes, it wasn't until three days later that we'd be able to venture back home to see what was left. Although I knew God was our everything, on a human level, it made me sick to my stomach to imagine what waited for us inside those walls.

I'll never forget the day we were allowed to return to our homes. The streets were coated with a sheen of filth that wafted into my nostrils and made my throat clench at the stink of destruction. We were in an apartment complex at the time, and every building we passed had been underwater. As we approached, the blistering heat and stifling humidity made it hurt to breathe. The thought of salvaging what might be left of our home's interior had me hesitant to shove the front door open. This was our home, and everything in it was a reflection of the life Ruthy and I had built together. But what would be left?

Poking my head inside while holding my breath, I yelled out. Ruthy didn't know why I had yelled, but she yelled too. It was funny because she does that. I couldn't believe what I was seeing. Our home was just as dry as the day we fled for our lives. How in the world could every apartment building in this huge complex get soaked and ours go untouched? It was straight God, of course. Say it with me. "That's crazzzzy." No, that's God.

God reminded me of the conversation we had on the rescue boat. It didn't matter if we'd lost everything, because we had not lost our relationship with God. We were going to be okay with whatever was lost or damaged inside our home because we'd escaped that killer storm with our lives, each other, and God's loving mercy.

In the months following Harvey, I couldn't shake thoughts of that storm and how it changed all our lives in unexpected ways. I remembered watching *The Wizard of Oz* as a kid and how that monster twister zigzagged across the Kansas landscape, kicking up dust and turning Dorothy's world upside-down. A passing thought. No big deal, right?

But one morning as I prayed in the quiet of my office preparing the Sunday message, *The Wizard of Oz* kept tugging at my spirit, but I didn't know why. It was an old movie, and it had nothing to do with that Sunday's Word. Still, I sat and lingered in prayer. Suddenly, God said, "When you pray, you're releasing heaven into the earth."

"Okay, Lord," I whispered.

His Word dropped into my spirit and settled there. I knew there was more coming, so I pressed in. Yet, nothing. I was like, what else you got for me, Father? But there was only the seed He'd planted: "When you pray, you're releasing heaven into the earth." You're releasing earthly cares for a heavenly reality.

God's got a great sense of humor and timing, so I wasn't surprised about having to wait for Him to fill in the rest of His revelation. It wouldn't come until the next Sunday. Can you imagine sharing a Word and then God jumping tracks to give you another Word? Yeah, that's exactly what happened that Sunday.

As I preached, the entire metaphor of the Yellow Brick Road came spilling out faster than I could contain it. I rolled with it as people began to clap, laugh, and shout, "Amen." I was so excited about what was coming out of my mouth that I was doing the same as the congregation.

Paving Streets of Gold

Revelation 21:21 tells us that in heaven, the streets are paved with gold: "The great street of the city was of gold, as pure as transparent glass." All right, here was the Yellow Brick Road, but how did it apply to our earthly lives, I wondered. Guided by the Holy Spirit, I found another clue in the book of James, where the apostle (and half-brother of Jesus) says that our tongue is powerful, like the rudder of a ship:

> Although [ships] are so large and are driven by strong winds, they are steered by a very small rudder wherever the pilot wants to go. Likewise, the tongue is a small part of the body, but it makes great boasts ... With the tongue, we praise our Lord and Father, and with it, we curse human beings, who have been made in God's likeness. Out of the same mouth come praise and cursing. My brothers and sisters, this should not be. Can both fresh water and salt water flow from the same spring?
> James 3:4-11 NIV

God showed me that when we pray, we release heaven—we essentially "pave" the earth with heaven's streets of gold. In my mind's eye, I saw the Yellow Brick Road, and suddenly, everything clicked.

As believers, we're called to "speak life" or to bring heaven down to earth through the Word of God. We should be walking on the Word, right? That means we pave the road before us just as heaven's streets are paved with gold—the Yellow Brick Road. We bring heaven into the earthly realm by the words we say and the words we pray. It's an exchange of wishes, our desire for his.

Remember the words of the Lord's Prayer? "Thy kingdom come, Thy will be done, on earth *as it is in heaven.*" Jesus intended those words to be so much more than a nice prayer we rattle off before communion. The Word of God is all-powerful and living, sharper than a two-edged sword. It changes the course of history. It transforms lives. It can even change a wretch like me. The question is, "Have you allowed it to do for you what it has done for me?"

I Was Lost, But Now I'm Found

Anglican clergyman John Newton said it best when writing the lyrics to "Amazing Grace." You see, as wretched as I was, I am now the perfect picture of God's amazing grace. Unless you know me personally, you might see this persona of a happy, joy-filled pastor who loves shoes, but the truth is that it took God's radical transformation to save me from myself.

I was a sower of death, and before my radical transformation for Christ, my joy came through stealing, killing, and destroying. However, by God's grace, he planted in me a deep, burning passion to sow life where death once prevailed. The life I live on purpose is for bringing His glorious light into the darkest of places—to pave the earth with heaven's streets of gold.

Instead of being busy with back-alley drug deals and criminal courtroom appearances, by the amazing grace of God, I purposely surrender my life to crusades for Christ and street revivals. What I've come to discover is that my testimony bears His great power throughout the world as it proclaims the truth of the Gospel. As a matter of fact, a testimony is a statement of a witness under oath, so this means that our testimonies actually bear proof of what God has done in our lives as we tell the story of how we overcame. In the pages ahead, I'll share my own testimony of God's grace and redemption.

Where Are You on the Yellow Brick Road?

As I continued meditating on the metaphor of the Yellow Brick Road, I discovered parallels within L. Frank Baum's story of Dorothy and *The Wonderful Wizard of Oz*. Throughout her journey from Kansas into Oz, Dorothy encounters three characters who each desperately long for something they don't have. Or you could say they each long to be changed. As Christians, we can view these characters as symbolizing three different things that we need to change within ourselves.

- One is looking for a brain.
- One is looking for a heart.
- One is looking for courage.

Allow me to whet your appetite for what's ahead with these corresponding words from Scripture:

Romans 12:2 – Do not conform to the pattern of this world but be transformed by the renewing of your **mind**. Then you will be able to test and approve what God's will is—his good, pleasing, and perfect will.

Ezekiel 36:26 – I will give you a new **heart** and put a new spirit in you; I will remove from you your heart of stone and give you a heart of flesh.

Joshua 1:7 – Be strong and very **courageous**. Be careful to obey all the law my servant Moses gave you; do not turn from it to the right or to the left, that you may be successful wherever you go.

As you will soon see, walking God's Yellow Brick Road (releasing heaven on earth by our prayers) will not only "grow you up" into the things of the Spirit, it will show you why you have been placed here for such a time as this—in essence, what your personal mission is as part of Christ's Great Commission.

Are you ready to take this journey with me? If so, then fasten your seat belt because things might get a little bumpy up ahead.

Remember, it all starts with a storm.

THROUGH THE STORM

GAINING PERSPECTIVE FROM THE PAIN

We all have a "storm story," so I want to share some sunshine by going tough love on you for a moment, but it's for your own good. I also want us to begin moving forward along the Yellow Brick Road, so it's important for you to understand that the mess you find yourself in is because you're complicating God's promise for your life.

Maybe you're going through that storm right now. Maybe it's an addiction or debt, or marriage problems, etc. Maybe you're going through life gripped by fear and doubt. Maybe you need healing from a past relationship, or there is sickness in your body. No matter what you're facing, there is only one way—one *road*, one Yellow Brick Road—to that place of God's promise.

We all have a storm story. As a matter of fact, rarely have I met a strong person who doesn't have one. I want to take you on a journey that will get you on the road to proclaiming God's promise for you regardless of where you are in life. We will get you an answer.

Singing in my best Dorothy voice, here goes: "And we're off to see the Wizard, the wonderful Wizard of Oz." Or, in this case, the wonderful Father of Heaven!

Count It All Joy

Maybe that's why James, the brother of Jesus, said to count it all as joy when going through various trials (see James 1:2-3). Contrary to what we might want to believe, the Bible never promises that we won't go through things. Quite the opposite, in fact.

> And the God of all grace, who called you to his eternal glory in Christ, after you have *suffered a little while*, will himself restore you and make you strong, firm, and steadfast.
> 1 Peter 5:10 NIV (emphasis added)

Did you catch that? He said "after you've suffered a little while."

If you're like the old me, you'd rather do without that part about suffering, thank you very much. But over the past few years, God has fast-tracked me and taken me on a whirlwind ride like nothing I could have ever dreamed up.

Are you familiar with the term "apprehend?" It's a word used in law enforcement, like when a police officer *apprehends a criminal.* It means to arrest, seize, grasp, or capture. Well, after living a life on the jagged edge for twenty years by dealing drugs and causing destruction everywhere I went, that's what God did to me. He *apprehended me—* grasped me out of a life racing headlong toward hell and put me on a new path. On this new path, I became like the blind man healed by Jesus. Yes, by His grace, I can say, "I don't know about all that, but one thing I do know. I was blind, but now I see" (John 9:25, paraphrased).

Remember the story I shared with you about sitting in the rescue boat and grieving over the thought of losing everything? Well, God brought my perspective back into alignment with truth: God is our everything. During a storm, we might think we are losing everything because we misplace our identity in things not of Christ; but in reality, we are not losing anything because these things are merely material possessions or a relationship that you shouldn't have gotten into.

At any moment, we could lose every material possession we have,

2

but we would still have our relationship with God. I'm sure most people would tell me they wouldn't have had thoughts like I did, but until you are faced with losing all your stuff, you don't really know what your perspective would be.

God uses situations in our life to remind us that He is everything. This was my proving ground, what I like to call a heart check, aka the test. God used the reality of losing everything during Hurricane Harvey to bring about a greater eternal perspective: He is everything in my life, and storms will always come and go.

In life, many times, we focus on the storm and what's on the outside when all that really matters is what's on the inside—the real you, the real me, and our relationship with the One who is bigger than any storm. God has shown me that every time I pray and release something from heaven, it paves the same road here on earth for making my path straight. So, every prayer I pray paves a road that orders my steps, like the lamp that is unto my feet (see Psalm 119:105). As I pray, I follow the direction of the road that is laid out before me, and I begin to walk in a way that leads me to the answer. That's what we call walking on the promises of God.

From Black-And-White To Technicolor

I love colors. That's the way God made me, and I'm thankful for that passion for fashion as well as the way colors move me. The distinction of colors used in *The Wizard of Oz* also moved me as I understood it to signify the different seasons in our lives. Sure, we have phases in life where our reality is the starkness of black-and-white, but once we come into an incredible relationship with Jesus Christ, there is a technicolor explosion of understanding God's truth.

When Dorothy experienced her transformation from an identity rooted in the limited life she only knew (filmed in black-and-white) and into the promise of a journey she was about to embark upon, the symbolism of color (Technicolor) shows the endless potential for moving forward and into the true knowledge of who she was created to be.

Are you living in a world where the words others speak over you remove God's beautiful colors from your life? Dorothy was similar in that she allowed people in her life to speak the "color" right out of her potential for joy. Even the people closest to Dorothy were anxious to point out her shortcomings. Someone told her she needed to use her brain to confront the problem she was running from. Another person said she just needed to have courage. And finally, her aunt pointed out that she was always worrying about something that was really nothing.

Isn't that like most of us? We get anxious over everything, yet pray about nothing. What mattered more than Dorothy's point being pondered was her process for approaching it. She allowed negative words to occupy her spirit and turn her colorful potential into a drab black-and-white reality. Dorothy, just like all of us, has a decision to make. How we approach those decisions can be just as important as the decision itself.

She, like we, face many opportunities to make decisions that will affect our internal reality. In her process of seeking truth, Dorothy begins to talk about a place where no trouble exists but that you couldn't get to with a boat or a plane. It was a place somewhere far away. It was a place somewhere over the rainbow.

I believe that "somewhere over the rainbow" signifies a promise she wanted to see come to pass. When I hear that song, I think about the cross. As believers, we want to see certain promises come to pass in our lives too. In fact, the life that God desires for each of us to have here on earth only comes by way of His promises. And His promises are *somewhere over the rainbow*, meaning they are in the heavenlies—but we have access to pull them down into our current situations. Through the power of prayer, the kingdom of God is at hand. And we have full access!

It gets better. Not only is the kingdom of God at hand, but He wants us to take hold of what He has already given us *now*. To do this, our perspective has to shift. Dorothy was dreaming of something far off, and all the while, it was a place that needed to exist in and through her. The Holy Spirit is here with us, and He is ready to do great things in and through our lives.

However, we have an adversary, the devil, who wants us to live in fear. The minute he tries to threaten us, most of us run away instead of confronting the lie or facing the giants of insecurity, fear, approval from others, addictions, selfishness, worry, etc. That means we're running away from things that we should be confronting.

As the storm approaches, Dorothy runs back to her farm and into the house, where she is hit in the head as her bedroom window is blown open. After she comes to, we glimpse her innermost thoughts and emotions. Images appear from the farm, and those who she loves most began to float by in the storm. Suddenly, she's confronted with a glimpse of what she fears the most—and it seems to take over the scene. Her fear needed to be confronted, but first, she had to see things differently.

She needed a perspective shift; she needed to reposition her thinking. If we are to take on a new perspective in life, we must let God into those innermost thoughts and emotions. Otherwise, the enemy will keep us bound with the emotion of fear.

I liken this transition to moving from black-and-white (believing a lie) to the Technicolor of truth. God's truth. I can tell you that when my own life transitioned from living the lies of the devil to sharing God's truths, it was as radical as seeing something dead come back to life

Storms: God's Agents Of Change

Why is it that we think storms are bad? Well, we hear of the destruction they bring, mostly from the media, but also from word of mouth. I want to invite you to look at storms with new eyes. In Luke 8:22-24, we read that Jesus said to His disciples, "Let's cross to the other side of the lake." So, they got into a boat and started out. As they sailed across, Jesus settled down for a nap. But soon, a fierce storm came down upon the lake. The boat was filling with water, and their perspective told them they were in real danger. The disciples woke Jesus up, shouting, "Master, Master, we're going to drown!"

When Jesus woke up, He rebuked the wind and the raging waves. Suddenly, the storm stopped, and all was calm. If we look at this story carefully, we see there's a storm, but I see a promise too. I see Jesus saying, *Let's go to the other side.* In other words, if Jesus said it that means no storm can stop you. The disciples should have remembered what Jesus said and told the storm to muzzle up; in other words, "Shut up, storm," knowing they were going to the other side. Let's stop complicating God's promises with our solutions!

Last I heard, Jesus took the sting from death. So why panic and freak out about a storm? After all, a storm isn't supposed to bring us to a bad place in our life, even if it leads to death. If we know that our end here on earth is only the beginning of our eternity with Jesus, why do we consider death such a bad thing? Now, don't think I'm suggesting that there should be no compassion or mourning for those who have passed on, but should we not celebrate someone going to glory? When someone dies, the real concern is whether he or she received salvation through faith in Jesus.

After spending much time in prayer and deep thought regarding storms and especially Hurricane Harvey, I went back to Genesis and thought about God and the beginning of time. When God spoke, His words filled the dark, void space with things created from the sound of His voice. I imagined trees coming up from out of the ground, the roaring tidal waves racing to find the shore, fire forming to fashion the sun, and earthquakes molding the landscapes of earth. I wondered about how galaxies came into existence and how planets were formed. I can't help but think that when God spoke, the atmosphere probably looked chaotic as each of these things was being created.

When I scale my life to all of creation, I laugh, realizing how we think our storms are bigger than the universe at times. I bet if we had a front-row seat to watch the birth of creation, we would have thought it was a storm of mass destruction when really, it was creation forming. God always brings something good from the storms in our lives. He brings creation from chaos.

What looked like a storm for us in Hurricane Harvey was the start of something new. God wanted to move me along to somewhere I would not have gone because I wanted to stay in my comfort zone. Sometimes a storm is just what we need. Every storm is an opportunity to encounter God or, as I like to say, to "Get Wrapped." Now, I am not saying that God causes the storms, but He will use a storm to bring about His plans and purposes. With that said, we shouldn't be so quick to call something bad that may not be bad at all. If I have in my mindset that a storm is bad, I might miss out on the opportunity to grow from it. Every storm is an opportunity to apply God's wisdom to a situation and grow, what we would call pass the test, and with every test we pass, we mature.

Who are we to judge good from bad anyway? Think about Jesus hanging on the cross. What looked like a horrific storm and imminent death to this man, whom so many came to love and believe, was the single most miraculous event in history, whereby the whole world was blessed. The devastation felt was nothing compared to the victory gained that day. Writing to the Corinthians, the apostle Paul said,

> But we speak the wisdom of God in a mystery, even the hidden wisdom, which God ordained before the world unto our glory: Which none of the [demonic] princes of this world knew: for had they known it, they would not have crucified the Lord of glory.
> 1 Corinthians 2:7-8 KJV

Satan thought he had killed the Anointed One, but God used the "storm" of Good Friday to complete His ultimate plan to save mankind through the death, burial, and resurrection of Jesus.

Out of Harvey, we wound up moving into an amazing neighborhood that is the best place I've ever lived. Furthermore, I was inspired to write this book, and I'm traveling and teaching leadership classes on a much bigger scale than before. Little did I know this storm would prove to be the perfect catalyst to send me from where I was to where I'm supposed to be now.

It wasn't the first time God used a storm to get my attention and redirect my course. Looking back over my life, I see His hand so clearly now, but that wasn't always the case.

THE STORM THAT HIT ME IN THE HEAD

BUT GOD HAD OTHER PLANS...

I grew up on Twelfth and Hudson in Hoboken, New Jersey. Although it was the low-income housing section, I was able to see the magnificent Manhattan skyline every time I hopped off the stoop. The Empire State Building and Twin Towers were a sight to see, but because they were right there in front of me, I never understood how amazing they really were, or why people came from all over the world just to see what I saw for free.

What I saw was truly incredible as I went on my way to hang out in the projects on Madison and Monroe Streets. Kids playing outside as fire hydrants spilled their relief from the sweltering days of summer, the grownups playing dominoes, and everyone slipping through their day to the sound of salsa. It was magical, and I basked in that enchanted atmosphere. Every day I dreamed of being "the man"—not just some loser, but the kind of guy other people looked up to and respected. Maybe even feared.

My parents, both from Puerto Rico, were Catholic by default. I'm not saying this was a bad thing, but nobody ever spoke to me about the importance of having a personal relationship with Jesus Christ. For me, Catholicism was mostly religion, an endless round of crucifixes, incense, and rules about what you could and could not do. It was impersonal, unlike the streets, which were filled with life and relationships.

As exciting, diverse, and alive as my hood was growing up, I still felt like an outsider. I was a puny kid, and while most Boricuas were darker with curly hair and brown eyes, I didn't look Puerto Rican. My blue eyes and lighter skin tone left most mistaking me as a white boy. For a young kid struggling to know who he was in the world, that created a critical identity crisis.

To make up for my shortcomings, I was determined to outdo everybody else. I always had to be the loudest, the funniest, the guy with the most money, and super flashy (lol). Absent a solid relationship with my father, or an understanding of who I was, I became obsessed with the lives of people on TV.

Characters like Scarface, the ruthless drug kingpin, appealed to me because I perceived his life as a fantasy that I desired to live in reality. He was flashy and had all the big parties while surrounded by the beautiful people who respected and feared him. I understand now that the father-son relationship void created a screwed-up perspective of what manhood should look like. But when you've got nothing, even the bad looks like something.

Growing into a positive identity is tough when surrounded by mixed messages and shaky foundations. When we buy in to what others say about us is when we set ourselves up for failure. Instead of realizing our identity through Christ, we struggle to please others in the confines of performance-based relationships.

For example, if you'd asked the people from my childhood, most would say I was a good kid. I played baseball, made good grades, and was outgoing. While that might've earned me a pat on the head from a nun in church, it wasn't reality. Inside, I was a wild child aching to bust loose. My rage was fueled by a failing home environment.

The moment my world actually crashed into pieces was the day I heard horrible screams coming out of my parents' bedroom. I was about eight at the time, and desperate shrieks caused fear to squeeze my chest until I could barely suck in a breath. I forced myself to look out of my room, although I was terrified of what I might see. My parents' voices were harsh and violent. I'd never heard anything so scary. Wobbly legs barely held me up as emotions washed over me, but I willed myself to sneak down the hall.

I saw my dad's strong grip snatch my mom by her long dark hair. It wasn't playful teasing. He jerked her by the head as she screamed and fought back. This couldn't be happening. I dearly loved both my mom and dad, so how could they not love each other? Still, I had to do something because the look on my dad's face showed his anger had boiled over and was at a point where he might've killed her. But I was only eight and so afraid. What could I do?

As the rage of anger replaced childish fear, I scrambled back into my bedroom. My watering eyes roamed wildly for something. Anything. There it was. My sweaty little fingers choked up on the Little League baseball bat as I hurried back into their room. I huffed in a breath and swung for the outfield fence as I blasted the aluminum pipe smack into my dad's right leg. It stunned him enough to let go of my mom, and I didn't care that he batted me across the room. All I knew was that I had to rescue my mom at any price.

While the violence might have stopped that day, it didn't bring peace. My mom walked out on my dad at that very moment. She made sure I understood that no one would ever hit either of us again. The family life I'd known of Mom and Dad had now been crushed into dust. From that day, my journey took a sharp turn downward.

I understood why my mom no longer wanted anything to do with my dad, but as a boy who desperately needed a dad, I wanted to see him more than ever. The problem with substituting TV for parenting is the fantasy of what happy families are supposed to look like. Even that became a source of pain as I watched caricatures of moms, dads, brothers, and sisters enjoying loving relationships across the airwaves of a false reality.

Finally, the isolation with my mom was too much, and I had to see him. I remember the day because my hero, my dad, was sitting in a dark room crying because my mom wasn't there. I wanted to hold him and hit him at the same time. Honestly, I didn't know what to feel. I was an empty shell who had no idea how to relate to someone in a healthy way.

As I gazed at his shaken frame, my mother's words echoed in my mind: "Son, you never let somebody hit you!" I still couldn't believe she'd just walked out that day. There was no second chance, no forgiveness, no nothing. While she was only trying to shield us from his abuse and show me her strength as a protector, I was pissed at her for keeping him out of my life.

Over time, the relationship with my dad morphed into an odd kind of friendship. Having him in my life, if even on a limited basis, still wasn't what I desired. I had enough friends; what I needed was a father. Besides stopping by and the checks he mailed in, it wasn't ever anything more than the minimum required by the state's visitation custody requirement.

In hindsight, my dad didn't suffer like I did. He actually enjoyed his freedom to live life as he chose. Sure, he'd break off a little of his time for me, but otherwise, he spent his life spending lots of money on lots of women. He always had parties. Lots of parties! Puerto Ricans sure do know how to party.

It was during that season that I began to move away from the idealistic TV fantasy families I wasted so much time watching with my mom and began to embrace the chauvinistic image of what my dad represented a macho man to be. In between those rare visits, his lifestyle captured my imagination. I wanted to be just like my old man. He had the best of both worlds. Just because he didn't live with us didn't mean he wasn't my dad, and he got the bonus of living the carefree life of a real man. Yeah, parties. Lots of parties.

We gain our first impressions of God the Father from our earthly dads. While I knew my dad, I didn't actually know him or anything about him. It was the same way with God the Father. I knew there was a God, but I knew nothing about Him. He was just some guy who was far off, that if I had an emergency, He'd come to my rescue.

I guess you could say that I knew *of* Him, but I didn't *know* Him. You see, not truly knowing Him, you can never partake of anything God has for you or for you to do. However, if I were to introduce you to Him and you were intentionally to develop the relationship, the possibilities of what you could do with Him and what He could do with you are limitless. I wish I knew back then what I know now, but I had no real personal relationship with God. I had no way of knowing that my identity needed to be found in Jesus Christ, so I was left to figure it out while trying to copycat the man I saw in my dad.

Satan had a field day with me. I was like an insect attracted to the deceptive light of a bug zapper. I was drawn to anything and everything, especially money, women, cars, and jewelry. Scarface was still my model of the ultimate alpha male, and my dad's wanton lifestyle only confirmed it. Yet no matter how much I attained, it was never enough. My thirst was becoming as big as the world. I guess these things temporarily filled the void and helped make me feel loved, secure, significant, and living for a purpose. It wasn't God's will or purpose for my life, though. It was my own, and it was destructive.

Author Ed Cole states, "Love is the desire to benefit others, even at the expense of self, because love desires to give. Lust is the desire to benefit self, even at the expense of others, because lust wants only to get. Love is easily satisfied; lust is insatiable. Love is the nature of Heaven, while lust is the nature of both a living and eternal Hell." Something within you that continues to scream, "More."

The Tipping Point

As if my life hadn't been screwed up enough, my mom decided to remarry. I can tell you that the guy she married had to be someone very special, because I wanted nothing to do with him. That was my mom, and if she wasn't going to be with my dad, then she shouldn't ever be with anyone else again. Of course, that made perfect sense to an eleven-year-old. Turned out Paulino was a good guy, and a relationship began to grow despite my resistance to him.

Kinda like Smalls' stepdad in *The Sandlot*, Paulino worked hard to support my passion for baseball. I'm not sure where the desire to play came from, but maybe it's a Puerto Rican thing. Hustling from practices to my games helped fill a dark void in my life, and no matter what Paulino did to help, it would never be enough. I wanted my dad there, and with every swing, throw, or stolen base, his absence hurt more and more.

I'd learned to suck up my hurt and swallow the lump in my throat every time I took my turn at bat. I recall squinting through the metal fence and into the crowd of parents in hopes of spotting the one man I wanted to be like and be with more than anything in the world—my dad. And you know, he was always consistent in that he consistently never showed up.

Life can be complicated. Instead of enjoying the childhood competition of Little League baseball, I was struggling with abandonment and the dual emotions each time I picked up a baseball bat. I never forgot that it was a similar bat I used to rescue my mom from my dad's physical abuse. Maybe the baseball bat represented my mom's freedom from my dad's physical abuse while also condemning me to a life without him.

It was during that time in my life that baseball and Paulino's best efforts both failed to keep me interested. One of the guys I played ball with had become a close friend. We'd connected over our respective father wounds. His dad had died when he was very young, so he also grew up wanting nothing more than a dad. That was a deep, dark bond that grew strong, and we soon spent most of our time hanging out. What started out with sharing McDonald's and secrets on the way to practice soon evolved into sharing drugs and alcohol.

Soon, all we did was hang out in the park drinking and smoking weed in the basements. Our crew of what we called free agents grew to mostly all guys without dads. We might've been free to do whatever we pleased, but this gang of boys without direction would've given up the dope for a dad any day. Can you see how plain and simple was the enemy's plan to attack all of us boys? Well, at that age and with zero parental guidance, it was easy pickings to slither in and stake his claim on our souls.

Yeah, the enemy had me pretty much wrapped up, all right. Smoking weed opened the door for selling mescaline by the time I was thirteen. It wasn't a year later that I got to know cocaine thanks to one of my friends. When using it wasn't enough, I started selling it as a high school freshman. Of course, once I had the taste for cash, I needed to expand my operation. My stepdad, Paulino, owned bars in the area, so I shifted my focus from high school kids to forty-something-year-old men.

What was worse, a teenaged boy selling coke or an adult buying dope from a teenaged boy? It didn't matter at the time because my life was an empty pit that required more money, risk, and power. Having people depend on me to supply them with what they wanted gave me that sense of power.

I recall the first time it hit me how crazy this whole good-life, bad-life game was. Some of the very same family members who faithfully attended church as good members of society were also my competitors in pushing dope. They put on pretty faces that told the world they had it all together when, just like me, their lives were spinning out of control. It was a crazy lifestyle that could only end in destruction.

The nuttiest part was that these same family members were the ones making the biggest show for God. They told others about Him, prayed in the open to Him, and claimed to live their lives for Him, but in truth, God was nothing more than a magic genie for granting wishes and keeping the cops away from their doors.

After that eye-opener, I felt like there was nothing attaching me to being that good kid I was once thought to be. I mean, if my family could play the dope game and love God, why couldn't I? By my senior year, I was doing things that most people would only see happen in a movie.

I don't want to glorify that lifestyle, so I'm deliberately not going into too much detail here. I'm giving you the PG version. In my mind, life was being lived out just like the movie *Belly* when DMX and Nas were walking into the club in slow motion to the song in my Soul II Soul voice "Back to Life." But in reality, I was destroying home after home and turning good kids into drug addicts.

I was becoming a master at my craft, but the attention I was drawing to myself caused drug investigators to hassle me every week. Besides the drugs and alcohol, I just enjoyed the attention of acting a fool. I know it's wrong, but one morning before school, my friend and I chugged a six-pack of Heineken beers at the front entrance. It was on a dare and to get much-needed attention from my peers. When you're hurting for affection, any affection will do.

That little act of rebellion would soon become another turning point in my life. While we were getting our buzz on, a school security guard caught on to what we were doing. He was crazy overweight, and when we'd yell out, "Hey Kool-Aid," the other students would scream out, "Oh yeah." Despite our disrespect for his size, his perseverance caught up to us.

The school administration basically liked me but were placed in the situation of having to make an example of me because of my bad behavior. I was told to skip senior prom, or else I wouldn't be allowed to walk the stage at graduation. You wouldn't think that'd be a hard call, but oh man, I loved a great party. My mom, on the other hand, made the decision easy—graduate or she'd kill me. Needless to say, I didn't go to the prom.

It's funny that I thought missing my prom was a big deal. It was nothing compared to the next bit of news from my senior year. I was going to be a dad. Yeah, you read that right—a dad. Right after graduating from high school, I realized the life I was living wasn't conducive to fatherhood. I was on the fast track to an orange jumpsuit in a state prison. I needed an out, and the United States Navy was going to provide it.

Still, I was looking for the structure I missed while growing up, and military discipline seemed like the answer. Also, desperate to make one right decision in life, I married the mother of my son, Juan (aka JJ). Talk about going from bad to worse. Neither of us was ready to be a spouse or a parent. And to top it all off, I sure wasn't ready for the military.

While the Navy helped mature me and introduced me to push-ups, lots and lots of push-ups, I was still the broken soul seeking to fill a vast void in my life. Wearing a uniform instead of civilian clothes didn't mean I changed who I was or what I did. Actually, my time in the service only helped introduce me to a much bigger view of the dark side of life.

Instead of growing in my responsibilities, I began hitting the clubs harder than ever before. I frequented major hotspots like Copa Cabana, Limelight (a church that became a nightclub), Studio 54, and Fox's. I was there every day and then hit the after-parties with mob strippers and soap opera stars who'd hang out and buy coke from us.

After my discharge, I had another opportunity to become the father my dad never was to me. I had a wife and son at home, but instead, I ran right back to my old friends. I might've even understood why my dad never tried to reconcile with my mom. I hated him for enjoying the single life while still pretending to be my dad, but here I was, doing the exact same thing.

It was no surprise we soon divorced. When you're living outside of God's will, life is never easy. After we divorced, I discovered she was pregnant with our second son, Jonathan. Remarriage wasn't an option. My heart yearned for the streets' grit and the nights' flash, not my sons' hugs.

Following A Crooked Pattern

I've learned that no matter how old you are and what you have experienced in life, if you do not heal the wounds of your past, you will keep stepping on the scabs. I was attracted to dysfunctional relationships like the junkies I kept fueled with dope.

My fresh start by moving to Virginia for a change of scenery and people just meant I would keep doing the same old stuff with new people in new places.

My third child, Janina, and second marriage had the same failed outcome as my first. What is it we say about insanity? It's doing the same thing over and over again while expecting different results.

I was living the double agent's life of pretending to be a husband and daddy while getting high and selling drugs behind her back. When she demanded I stop, that old selfish desire overcame me, and just like my dad had shown me, I chose to abandon them both because they cramped my style.

Back on my own and without even the slightest moral compass, life continued spiraling beyond my control. The drugs, sex, and life of violence began to catch up to me, and so had the cops. Did someone say, "Texas"?

Way Down In Texas Way

I'm a natural entrepreneur, so when I learned about a hot new drug market busting open just across the Texas/Mexico border, I had to be a part of it. I knew there were several factors driving me.

I still had to be the flashy guy, being the "man" meant everything to me, and failing as a father shoved me to restart my life over and over again where I could hide from the past by remaking myself into whoever I thought I was destined to be. Texas would be my fresh start, as well as my chance to vanish from my kids and conceal my failure.

Remember what I said about repeating bad patterns in life? Well, as you might've guessed, I dove headfirst into the big-time world of drug trafficking. Known as "New York J," I was on the verge of becoming the top dog in a dusty Texas town.

It was during a stint in one of the most dangerous prisons that I finally made the real-deal connections to become the Scarface I'd always idolized. Unfortunately, this once-innocent town was being demolished, and I was the guy swinging the wrecking ball.

What I hadn't bothered realizing was that it was my personal life that had been wrecked. It had been almost fifteen years since I'd spoken to any of my children, and my parents weren't sure if I was alive or dead.

Despite the damage to myself and others I took pride in causing, I found a perverse pleasure in attending church. I was still treating God like my back-pocket bottle genie.

I knew my life was destined for an early grave, so going to church seemed my best bet for avoiding the only thing I feared—hell. It was too bad I couldn't see that was where I was living and a place I had created for countless other addicts.

A Cry Of The Heart

After another bid in what started to be my second home, I walked out of jail and right back to the only thing I'd known since childhood. Still operating on gut instinct and the fantasy of the Scarface model of manhood, I connected with a new supplier for selling meth. As usual, it wasn't long until I was flush with cash and looking for a bigger score. What I thought was a big opportunity to score a huge supply had us on our way to Fort Worth so I could spend the giant wad of money in my pocket.

I guess looking back, I'm not surprised that instead of a fat batch of methamphetamine, I was greeted by a group of guys with ski masks and guns. They beat me like a dog for what seemed like an eternity. When their fists and feet stopped smashing into my curled-up punching bag of a body, it fell silent. It was an ink-black night, and I recall being glad that it was over. I'd survived their best beating and knew I'd get a ride back home to start amassing my fortune all over again. Except...

In the quiet of that night, I felt the hard thump against the back of my skull. Next, the distinctive cocking of a semiautomatic weapon preparing a bullet to be blasted into my head. In all the years from a dysfunctional childhood, military service, failed fatherhood, and life on the razor's edge of dealing drugs, never once was I afraid of dying. On my belly in the middle of nowhere with a loaded pistol pressed into my skull, I cried out to the Lord for the first time in my life. Desperate to stay alive, I recited the Lord's Prayer by yelling at the top of my lungs.

"Our Father, who art in heaven, hallowed be Thy name!" I shouted into the night air. "Thy kingdom come, Thy will be done, on earth as it is in heaven..."

About halfway through the prayer, I felt the pressure fade as the cold steel barrel was removed from my head. The squealing car tires and revving engine told me that they'd hurried off. Had they seen the cops? No, they, like me, had seen the light. They had intentions to stop my appointed destiny in the kingdom, but God had different plans. God had a calling on my life that I never saw. I didn't understand God as my Father because I'd always been so wrapped up in the broken relationship with my own dad. I looked at God the Father the same way I saw my dad. Very distant, uncaring, and not worried about me in the least bit. Boy, was I wrong.

You know the crazy thing about being in a rut is that you never get to really see what else is on the other side. Despite God's mercy in saving my life that night, all I knew to do was what I'd always done—sell drugs. The only people I had in my life were those who wanted to buy dope from me or kill me. So when I found myself alive after an assassination attempt, I crawled right back to the very guy who tried to have me killed in Fort Worth. Why did I go back? Because of the drugs. Why didn't he wrap up the job of having me killed? Because of God.

Rational people try to make sense out of irrational people's insane decisions, but it's not anything you can understand unless you've lived it. And I do not recommend you try that life just so you can understand the mindset. An occasion that even I still cannot figure out was once I was back in my drug supplier's "good graces," he decided we needed to have a talk. He sat down across from me with a loaded shotgun laid across his lap and shared the Gospel with me. I never stopped to think about the reality of going to hell for the life I was living. It was nuts, but he was the only person in all my years of living in the Bible Belt to ever tell me the truth of the Gospel.

While back on the streets selling drugs, I had a surreal moment that I remember like it was yesterday. Oddly enough, I was completely sober. We were heading toward Weatherford, Texas, and as I looked out the car window at the clouds, it was almost as if the clouds were speaking to me. It might sound weird, but I was so touched that I started crying. I wept uncontrollably. If you've been baptized in the Holy Spirit, you know what I'm talking about. It was that kind of cry.

The driver started freaking out because I was wailing out of control. We had a ton of meth on us, and I'm looking all crazy in the passenger's seat. In that moment, I heard something in my spirit that forever changed me. A still small voice said, "Why are you destroying the very lives I am giving people?"

"I'm sorry, God, I'm sorry…" I blubbered as the girl driving glanced at me, thinking I'd lost my marbles, also probably thinking we were going to jail.

The voice continued, "You're turning moms into prostitutes and taking men away from being fathers. You are destroying homes, cities, and states."

By then, I was a complete slobbery mess, and my driver was trying to talk to me all the while I was crying and apologizing. In what seemed like slow motion, she asked me, "What's wrong? What are you doing?" Then, in the twinkling of an eye, it was all over. The crying stopped, and all the tears dried up.

In that moment, I felt caught up in a whirlwind, just like Dorothy in *The Wizard of Oz*. Little did I know that this storm was coming so I could be taken to a place I had never known, a place I had always desired deep down. This unforeseen storm ultimately took me to the very place where I could finally find my answer to life—the *real me*.

3

GOD USES STORMS TO GET YOUR ATTENTION

ARE YOU LISTENING?

When the Bible speaks of something as being "good," the Hebrew word *Tov* is often used. *Tov* means "in its place, doing what it's supposed to be doing." On the contrary, *Ra* means not doing what a thing or person is supposed to be doing. It's obvious to see that when God uses a storm, His intention is to bring order from chaos and to bring us into alignment with our assignment.

In my crazy life, God used a storm to get my attention. What turned out to be my own Damascus Road experience included three very different roads: the night I almost got killed, God speaking to me from the clouds, and later making me a "new creation" in prison (you'll read about that later).

Think about the areas of chaos in your life and consider how God might use these storms to bring about a much-needed change. I was caught in storms called drug addiction, lust, and anger, as well as prison, and God used each of these chaotic situations to bring me closer to my purpose. Now, I'm not saying we should go out and create these storms to give God something to work with. Understand that we have free will, and with that comes great responsibility, and we will be held accountable for our choices. However, God will use our mistakes and our circumstances to bring about His greater plan and glory.

What is God speaking to you out of your current circumstances? The truth is, God is *always* speaking, and He desires to get your attention. Ever notice how God will use a person, social media (Facebook, Twitter, Instagram, etc.), or even a random sign to get His message across to you? If so, do you ignore it, or are you receptive and ready to listen? He's talking to you right now in RED letters. He loves you.

We respond to trouble and pain in the same way Dorothy tried to run away from the storm. After all, who really wants to go through a storm? Wouldn't we rather be magically transferred to a place where there is no trouble and be free of pain? God, on the other hand, uses these storms to take us through difficult times so that we can be refined in the fire. It's in those times that our transformation becomes central to becoming the person God wants to use for leading others to Him. Dorothy finds herself in so deep that she gets smacked in the head and ends up opening a window where she can see all the things flying around in her life. She even gets a glimpse of what she must confront, and she winds up in a place called Oz.

Every storm we endure leads to an opportunity to grow deeper in our faith. We learn that God can be trusted, so instead of running from howling winds, we hold onto His hand for the journey. In the midst of Dorothy's storm, she was given a glimpse of a life she could only dream about. But because she feared the storm would destroy her, she abandoned that desired life. Similar to the way God makes a path before us, Dorothy's storm didn't harm her but instead removed her obstacles. What the enemy meant for evil, God uses for good. Think about it: a house that got caught up in the same storm that took Dorothy to a place where she was able to help so many people also *crushed* the wicked witch.

At first sight, Dorothy was upset about the aftermath of the storm (seeing the witch crushed beneath the house), but when the Munchkins thanked her for freeing them, she had a greater understanding of what good came out of her personal storm. The results of Dorothy's storm were the real miracle. The people even proclaimed, "From now on, you'll be history, and we will glorify your name!"

Has God used your storms in life not only bless to you but also to be a blessing to so many others?

There is so much symbolism to be seen here. I see the Emerald City as heaven and Dorothy's ruby-red slippers as the blood of Jesus. The blood of Jesus gives us access and restores us to the original plan, or path, if you will. What a parallel to the storyline, right? After all, it was only after receiving the ruby slippers that Dorothy began following the Yellow Brick Road. When we come to the cross, we begin to follow the streets of heaven on earth. Later, we see how the ruby slippers gave Dorothy access to the city and to meeting the Wizard as well.

Equipped For His Purpose

I believe that when God created us, He equipped us with everything we could ever need. Let's say that you go into Home Depot to get a super awesome refrigerator. By the way, I want one of these super awesome refrigerators. So you go into Home Depot and see a refrigerator with all the bells and whistles; it has everything you could think of—even tells you if there's any milk in the fridge when you're not home.

The refrigerator costs thousands of dollars, you buy it, and that evening, they deliver it. You go to the store and buy ice cream, vegetables, and a few other items to place in the new refrigerator. You go to sleep and then wake up in the morning only to find that the ice cream is melted, and everything in the fridge is looking wilted and ugly, definitely not the way it's truly intended to look.

Oh no! You call Home Depot in a fury, saying, "Yo, I bought this refrigerator, and it doesn't work!"

The salesman says, "Now, calm down, sir, let's check a few things before we say that it's not working. Go put your ear to the refrigerator and tell me what you hear."

You mumble something in reply, open the refrigerator door to check the light…and nothing. The guy tells you to check the back of the refrigerator and see if the cord is plugged in. You go look, and guess what? It's not plugged in. Back at the phone, you tell the guy, "Hey, I know it's not plugged in, but for thousands of dollars, it shouldn't have to be. It should have worked."

The salesman explains that the new refrigerator has all the best parts and is designed to do and be all that it's cracked up to be—but not without power. The parts, as expensive and special as they are, won't do what they were made to do without being connected to the power. Thank you, Dr. Tony Evans, who gave an illustration like this in a sermon, and I have now made it my own (lol).

Second Peter 1:3 (NIV) states, "His divine power has given us everything we need for a godly life through our knowledge of him who called us by his own glory and goodness." When I think about the intelligence of God in creating us, why would He ever create us and not provide everything we need? You were wonderfully and fearfully made. He created you to be unique and special, a one-of-a-kind.

Think about this: when you were born, you already possessed the capabilities to ride a bike, drive a car, sing a song, jog, and even get married. The issue was that your skill sets had not yet developed, and to do those things, you needed to mature. I believe this ties in to how we develop spiritually. It's a process of development. As we read the Word and get to know Him, we mature and begin to walk in the way that He destined for us to. Please remember that development is a process, not an event. We grow daily, not in a day! Salvation happens in a moment, but it takes a lifetime to manufacture a saint.

Do you immediately go to God in prayer when tough times occur, or when He's trying to show you the areas of your life that are out of whack and need an alignment? We say, "Pray for clarity," yet the first place Dorothy came to while following the Yellow Brick Road was a fork in the road. As we follow the path laid out before us, we will often find ourselves at a crossroads of decision. That's why it is important to pray.

When we were baby Christians, any prayer would do, but as we grow in the Word, we need to learn how to pray with accuracy. To do that, we need to pray according to God's will with a good understanding of who He is. If you know God's will, but you're not sure of His character, then you might know He can do something, but you will question whether He wants to. We grow mature by being intimate with Him and His Word to grow to deeper levels of spiritual understanding. We cannot pray prayers that have no aim or substance. An old Chinese proverb states, "If you aim at nothing, you will hit nothing." Learn to pray with wisdom and strategy, with AIM, from the heart of God.

A Prophet With A Story

Look at what Isaiah 43:14-19 says regarding the "storm" that Israel found herself caught up in for some time:

This is what the Lord says—your Redeemer, the Holy One of Israel: "For your sake, I will send Babylon and bring down the Babylonians, in the ships in which they took pride. I am the Lord, your Holy One, Israel's Creator, your King." This is what the Lord says—he who made a way through the sea, a path through the mighty waters, who drew out the chariots and horses, the army and reinforcements together, and they lay there, never to rise again, extinguished, snuffed out like a wick: "Forget the former things; do not dwell on the past. See, I am doing a new thing! Now it springs up; do you not perceive it? I am making a way in the desert and streams in the wasteland."

Isaiah was telling the people of Israel the story of how God delivered them out of the grips of Egypt and Pharaoh. He was telling his hearers about how God had delivered them in the past, but in verse 18, he then tells them to forget all that. The point was that Israel needed to be delivered, but they needed to be open to God moving in a different way than expected. They expected God to deliver them in the same ways as in the past, but God was telling them to forget how He did it before. Yes, God planned to deliver them, but if they were looking for Him to do everything the same way He did in the past, they would completely miss the new way He had in store for them.

People and circumstances vary in every situation, and God will use different ways at different times. Often, when we are trying to honor the testimony of what God did in the past so that we can see it come to pass again, we get caught up in the method. If our focus is only on the method God used in our last circumstance, we will miss out on the way He is moving now because it might look different from what we expected.

Consider this: Isaiah is talking directly to you, and he is attempting to pump you up while you are in the midst of an intense spiritual battle. He soon persuades you to start singing "No Longer Slaves," and you reminisce about how God split the sea so that you could walk right through it. He's also emphatic about how the people who were in hot pursuit of you (to take you back and enslave you all over again) were drowned, while you got away on dry land. Then, at the height of your excitement, Isaiah asks if you are ready for God to do it again, and you shout "Yes!"—to which Isaiah replies, "Good, but you need to forget about how He did it in the past because God isn't going to bring you out the same way as before." In chapter 43 of Isaiah, he actually declares that God is doing something different. Instead of splitting the sea to create a dry place to walk through, God is making a path in the desert and will bring about streams of living water along the way to sustain you.

Could it be possible that in many areas of our lives, we get caught up in how God did something, and we expect Him to do it the same way again? When we look at the old way, we will miss out on the new way and even the revelation that comes with it. We would do well to stay open to how He decides to work things out.

Our Father is a good Father, and He has the perfect solution for the storm you are in. It just may look a whole lot different from what you were expecting, what you are used to, or even how your friend says it was for him. Don't miss out on a blessing because it isn't packaged the way you thought it should be.

Every person's testimony is unique to them, and every situation we experience is unique—that means different from the one before. Therefore, we cannot run with someone else's testimony, hoping it works for us. We also cannot bank on God doing the same thing over and over in our situations. God always does the right thing, even if it seems crazy, even if we don't understand it. People usually say, "That's crazy!"

I say, no, that's God!

And always—ALWAYS—we are required to choose: will we trust Him or not?

4

IF I ONLY HAD A BRAIN

OBTAINING THE MIND OF CHRIST

The Yellow Brick Road wasn't a straight line into the Emerald City, and a lot of times our journey into the promises of God is the same. In other words, on our way to the promised land, we all have a wilderness experience that shows us who we are.

It represents a transitional season, not where you used to be, but not where you want to be. It's about you beating you. All Dorothy wanted was to get home, yet she ended up having to go through areas that revealed things about herself that she needed to walk through and conquer.

The Yellow Brick Road led her to places that required her to make decisions to win the victory that was already hers all along.

In one of the first crossroads she comes to, Dorothy meets someone who "needs a brain," and she must make an intentional decision about which direction she will choose. Later, she runs into someone along the path who claims he "needs a heart," and she has to show compassion.

Shortly after that, Dorothy must get past her fears and stand up to someone who needs courage or "nerve." In each situation, she is forced to find within herself what is missing.

The Need To Choose

Let's look at the first character Dorothy encounters on the Yellow Brick Road—the Scarecrow. Standing at a crossroads, *she must choose which way she will go.* I love James 1:6-8 in the Passion translation: "Just make sure you ask empowered by confident faith without doubting that you will receive. For the ambivalent person believes one minute and doubts the next. Being undecided makes you become like the rough seas driven and tossed by the wind. You're up one minute and tossed down the next. When you are half-hearted and wavering, it leaves you unstable. Can you really expect to receive anything from the Lord when you're in that
condition?"

The trouble with the Scarecrow is that he can't make up his mind; he is double-minded. He even points his arms in both directions, as if that might help Dorothy and Toto. Here Dorothy is, already confused about which way to go, and I believe the Scarecrow represents our inability to make up our mind. He is aware of his shortcomings and confesses that he needs a brain. Picture the scene. When Dorothy comes upon the Scarecrow, he is stuck on the top of a pole, firmly grounded in the fork of the road, unable to confidently point Dorothy in the right direction.

When Dorothy lets him down, the straw that filled him falls out, and they both work to get it shoved back into place again. Without the renewing of our mind, we are stuck in confusion, with a life of no purpose. We are empty and void without form. Jesus is the only One capable of filling that void and forming us into who we were created to be. So many of us try to fill ourselves with all sorts of things that don't belong, lies taught to us by a godless society. Our flesh is never satisfied, and we constantly try to fill, refill, and replace things back into our lives that don't belong. We have to reposition our thinking. Until we understand what God is revealing to us through His Word, we'll stay stuck in indecision just like the Scarecrow was stuck on his pole.

Writing from Corinth on his third missionary journey, the apostle

Paul addressed a long letter to the church in Rome—a church made up of Jews and former pagans who now served the living God:

> Therefore, I urge you, brothers and sisters, in view of God's mercy, to offer your bodies as a living sacrifice, holy and pleasing to God—this is your true and proper worship. Do not be conformed to the pattern of this world but be **transformed by the renewing of your mind.** **Then you will be able to test and approve what God's will is**—His good, pleasing and perfect will.
> Romans 12:1-2 NIV

Think for a moment about what these believers in ancient Rome faced every day. Their city overflowed with temples to pagan gods, many of whom demanded "worship" in the form of sexual perversion with temple prostitutes. Paul was telling these believers, "But you are different! You are set apart! Don't be transformed to the pattern of this world but be transformed by the renewing of your mind…"

The Roman believers had to *choose* a new pattern—not the pattern of the world, but the God-printed pattern that emerged as they renewed their minds through hearing the Word. It comes from the word *cosmos*, which means thought patterns and trends, so don't think and trend like the world, but renew your mind to a heavenly mindset so that you can see clearly what God desires.

Let us remind ourselves that we are citizens of Heaven. I like to say, "We Are Heavicans." We should look like the place we are from, kind of like America=Americans, Puerto Rico=Puerto Ricans, Mexico=Mexicans, Africa=Africans, Heaven=Heavicans; you get it? Our culture is Heaven, and we build the kingdom on earth.

Let's look at our thinking as a pattern. As I mentioned earlier, to change the product (or result), you need to change the pattern. If we truly want to see lasting change in our life, we need God's thoughts to transform our thoughts and thus change the pattern of our thinking. Too many people want to go to church to be entertained or pleased. What we should be looking for is to encounter God's word in order to be changed. The thoughts of God are something we need to grasp from beyond our natural view. To do this, it will take God's Word to renew your mind and His Spirit to reveal the truths thereof.

Getting In Step With Agreement

Another key aspect of Dorothy's journey down the Yellow Brick Road is that every time she meets someone new, they have to get in step with her before they can start walking along with her. Dorothy makes sure that as they start out on their journey together, they are in step—or you could say in agreement—on the purpose of their journey together. Here we see that agreement is vitally important.

> I ask you, can two walk together unless they have agreed to do so?
> Amos 3:3 NIV

I remember moments when I struggled because of the void in my life. I tried to fill it with everything that brought me comfort, anything I thought would give me peace—women, drugs, being "the man." It was a false peace, temporary and not eternal.

When I was growing up, a TV commercial used to say the mind is a terrible thing to waste, and boy, was that accurate. As a believer, the mind is very important. Let's look at Philippians 4:8-9:

> Finally, brethren, whatever is true, whatever is honorable, whatever is right, whatever is pure, whatever is lovely, whatever is of good repute, if there is any excellence and if anything worthy of praise, dwell on these things. The things you have learned and received and heard and seen in me, practice these things, and the God of peace will be with you.

In other words, whatever you're thinking about will either bring you peace or chaos. Today, as a believer in Jesus Christ, I choose peace —the real peace that surpasses all understanding. But even as believers, we are constantly bombarded with thoughts, so I must choose to keep my mind in alignment with heaven. Yes, bad thoughts always come, but the Bible says we demolish, destroy strongholds—what's that? That means destructive thought patterns that lead people away from the things of God to hold them hostage to addictive behaviors, so instead of us being in a hostage situation being held by lies, we hold every thought captive to obey Christ and experience freedom by the knowledge of God's word, which is the truth that sets us free. Remember, it's a process, and the saving of your soul (mind, will, and emotions) is progressive; I promise it gets easier. All we are doing is building a relationship with the living and written Word.

Releasing Heaven On Earth

In our lives, as we follow the Yellow Brick Road—as we pray to release heaven on earth—we are essentially walking out the Word of God, and this is the only way we can truly overcome. Revelation 12:11 says that we overcome by the blood of the Lamb and the word of our testimony. The Word is really His Word. It's not just me saying, "I used to be addicted to drugs, and now I'm free."

One day as Jesus spoke in the Temple courts in Jerusalem, He said to the people who believed in Him, "If you hold to my teaching, you are really my disciples. Then you will know the truth, and the truth will set you free" (John 8:31-32 NIV). It's out of our being that we *do*. I was made free by spending time in His Word and through interacting with His Word. Just as John 8:36 says, "If the Son sets you free, you will be free indeed." Jesus and His Word make us free. However, it's up to us to walk according to His Word for that freedom to be truly experienced in our lives. In other words, we can't just talk about it, we must live it, and we can only live it by dying daily at the cross and allowing His spirit to live in our daily choices. Every *yes* to a promise of God is a *no* you have to say to the flesh.

Look at what God instructed Moses to tell the people of Israel before they entered the Promised Land. He knew they would encounter temptations and decisions, and they would *have to choose*. God wanted His people to remain separate or "set apart." He wants the same thing for us today:

Fix these words of mine in your hearts and minds; tie them as symbols on your hands and bind them to your foreheads. Teach them to your children, talking to them when you sit at home and when you walk along the road, when you lie down and when you get up. Write them on the doorframe of your houses and on your gates, so that your days and the days of your children may be many in the land that the Lord swore to give your forefathers, as many as the days that the heavens are above the earth.

Deuteronomy 11:18-21 NIV

All throughout Scripture, we are told to continually speak the words of God as we walk our lives. We see Jesus quoting such in the New Testament and hear about how the early church lived this out. Author and clergyman E.M. Bounds said, "The Word of God is food by which prayer is nourished and made strong." We are to pray and walk out the promises of God in our lives and the lives of those following after us. We pray the Word and take each step as it becomes illuminated. That's how we get through the storms in our lives and into the promises of God.

Isn't it interesting that the Scarecrow, who needed a brain, the Tin Man, who needed a heart, and the Lion, who needed courage, were all at different places along the path? The Scarecrow wasn't effective in what he was called to be, and he believed he wasn't able to think. Have you ever felt this way? Do you feel ineffective, or do you have a hard time believing that your mind is valuable? Do you ever feel like you're not smart enough? I know that was one of my storms. I felt like I was dumb and not smart enough until I realized I could ask God for wisdom, and because we are connected, I'm a genius by default (lol). And then the Tin Man got stuck. Could it be that the Tin Man stopped off at the fork in the road after he decided he needed to busy himself with all the work that needed to be done? In essence, he lost heart to continue advancing down the road.

We see that the Lion is farther down the road than any of the others. Even after he made the decision from his heart to stay on the path, what caused him to lose his courage and stop the journey? Many times, we make a decision, and we have it in our heart to continue on, but we sometimes still fail to keep our courage because we become afraid of what might happen if we actually get what we are seeking. It takes courage to keep going, especially when you don't yet see the fulfillment of the promise you are believing for. It takes a lot of nerve to keep moving forward: praying, staying in the Word, and walking out the steps that God places before us.

What words of God have you stopped praying over your life? Can you pinpoint where you might have jumped off the Yellow Brick Road? Are you in a place frozen with hopelessness while chopping wood? When did you allow indecision to halt your progress forward? Are you stuck like the Scarecrow, nailed to the post of "analysis paralysis"? Did you stop walking the path because of fear and a lack of courage?

Be Strong And Courageous

After Moses died, God began to talk to Joshua about taking Israel into the Promised Land. God tells Joshua three times, in Joshua 1:6-9, to be "strong and courageous." Think about this. God is taking all of them into the Promised Land, a land flowing with milk and honey. We must realize that this is the land Israel had waited forty years to get into, and just as they are about to experience the fulfillment, God says to Joshua, "Be strong and courageous."

Be strong and courageous, because you will lead these people to inherit the land I swore to their forefathers to give them. Be strong and very courageous. Be careful to obey all the law my servant Moses gave you: do not turn from it to the right or to the left, that you may be successful wherever you go.

Do not let this Book of the Law depart from your mouth; meditate on it day and night, so that you may be careful to do everything written in it. Then you will be prosperous and successful.

Have I not commanded you? Be strong and courageous. Do not be terrified; do not be discouraged, for the Lord your God will be with you wherever you go.

Joshua 1:6-9 NIV

This journey into a fulfilled promise definitely isn't for wimps or scaredy-cats. The journey is for those whose hearts are full of courage. It's for those who continually speak the Word and make intentional decisions. If you are going to come out of the storm and bring others out with you, you must stay the course with a courageous determination.

You must be like Joshua and Caleb, who saw the Land, who trusted and believed God. They were not moved by the giants or storms; they knew that if God was for them, then who or what can be against them. The truth is you will never get free by accident. God didn't tell Joshua not to worry about anything or that He would deliver all the people while he wandered around living life haphazardly. No, Joshua was called to live his life intentionally, every day, to see the promise that God had before him and all of Israel. Do you see clearly?

A Divine Intervention

Before God apprehended me, I was living my life intentionally, all right, but it was the wrong kind of intention. I was on a fast track toward hell. Sometimes I think God looks down from heaven at His future sons and daughters—the really tough cases like a Saul of Tarsus —and plots these dramatic interventions (storms) to turn them around so He can use them for His purpose.

Here was Saul, a "Pharisee of Pharisees," thinking he was doing God a favor by running around ordering the deaths of anyone caught following *The Way.* What way, you ask? The way of Jesus Christ. Saul's zeal was such that he was a man on a mission; he dedicated his life to killing Christians, the movement that was started by a man who had died in the end, hung on a cross between two criminals.

Sure, some whispered that this man Jesus rose from the dead, but Saul, along with most of the Pharisees, knew there had to be a practical explanation: most likely, his band of followers stole the body from the tomb and claimed a "resurrection from the dead." This couldn't be real, could it?

Acts 9:1 says Saul was "breathing out murderous threats against the Lord's disciples." After hearing rumors that these Way zealots were turning the city of Damascus upside-down, Saul obtained letters from the high priest authorizing him to arrest any followers of Jesus in Damascus. So he started out on the journey from Jerusalem, riding horseback with his companions, never dreaming what awaited him on the road up ahead.

On that road to Damascus, a blinding light struck down Saul and his travel companions. The guy was literally knocked off his horse. I don't know about you, but that would freak me out. Not only that, but Saul heard a voice say, "Saul, Saul, why do you persecute me?" (Acts 9:4 NIV). When Saul asked who was speaking, the voice replied: "I am Jesus, whom you are persecuting. Now get up and go into the city, and you will be told what you must do" (Acts 9:5-6 NIV).

It gets even worse for Saul; now, he realizes he can't see. You could say he was *blinded by the light.* They led him into Damascus to a man named Judas, who lived on—get this—Straight Street (you can't make this stuff up, right?). For three days, Saul was blind and didn't eat or drink anything.

Meanwhile, a disciple in Damascus named Ananias had a vision in which Jesus told him to go visit Saul. God would send people to you to accomplish His mission. Ananias was afraid because he knew Saul's reputation as a persecutor of the church. Jesus explained that Saul was His chosen instrument to deliver the gospel to the Gentiles, and so Ananias found Saul at Judas's house, just as Jesus showed him in the vision. Ananias laid his hands on Saul, asking the Lord to restore his sight and to fill him with the Holy Spirit.

The book of Acts says something like scales fell from Saul's eyes, and he could see again. He arose and was baptized into the Christian faith. After his conversion, Saul, which means "big one," changed his name to Paul, which means "little one." He had been a big shot for

God, or so he thought; now he considered himself a nobody for Jesus. We call that humility.

Before the Lord apprehended me, I sure thought I was a big shot— New York J, the fast-moving city guy who could have anything he wanted with a snap of his fingers. And like Saul, I was a tough case. God had a special intervention in store for me. Not just the miracle answer to my cry for help on a lonely Texas road at night. Not just His way of speaking to me through the clouds to tenderize my heart and prepare it for something new.

No, this special intervention—this storm—can be summed up in one word, and I thank God every day that He saw fit to use me for such a time as this.

That word is *prison.*

5

GOODBYE, NEW YORK J
THE IRON BARS OF FREEDOM

Shortly after God spoke to me, some guy pinned my name to a robbery that I had no part in. The guy was doing drugs with a prostitute when someone struck him in the head before robbing him. The woman claimed it was me, New York J. A quick call to the cops and his claim had me as their top suspect. I'll admit to having done lots of stupid stuff in my life, but robbing that guy was not one of them. Besides, I was in the clear because I'd been in another city at the time and had four witnesses to prove my innocence.

After talking with detectives, I decided to drive back home to clear my name. As we entered the city, I noticed surveillance vehicles everywhere. Have you ever seen cars on the side of the road with signs that read "For Sale?" Well, those weren't cars for sale. Like, even the hot dog vendor across the street was an FBI agent, you feel me?

The minute I pulled in and got out of my car, badges came out from everywhere. I was busted! I got caught red-handed with only a few grams of meth in my possession, but they weren't interested in the dope. They wanted me for the aggravated robbery. A conviction would mean a twenty-five-year prison sentence. As the justice system played out, the truth showed where I was, and my conviction was four years instead of a quarter of a century behind bars.

This time, I wound up incarcerated in Weatherford, Texas. Here I was, a Puerto Rican from New York, in the same cell with guys from the Aryan Brotherhood. As crazy as it sounds, this is where my life took a drastic change. I started reading *Faith to Faith* by Kenneth Copeland, and one day, I fell to my knees for the first time and had a real conversation with God.

The reality is, God was always talking to me, but although I had moments of hearing Him loud and clear, my pain kept cutting into our conversations, and I'd crawl back to the life that I thought was what being a man meant. The last time God had spoken so clearly was in the car when I started sobbing at His Words. Although I hadn't heeded His call, the words He spoke over me always tugged at my heart. That day in the cell, after reading Copeland's book, I was at the end of my rope. I needed to be saved, and finally, I realized that I couldn't do it on my own. There was no sermon being preached. No worship team. No theatrics. Just me begging God to save me.

Divine Appointment

While I was at Weatherford, I had several divine appointments. Where I was housed, there was this cage with a gated separation down the middle. One day, a guy walked to the gate and said, "Hey, I'm here for you."

This took me by complete surprise. No one had ever said that to me before. He told me he was incarcerated but that he was innocent. He was actually a pastor. At this time in my life, I had no idea what a pastor was. In Catholicism, there were only priests.

"You're a pastor?" I answered, hoping he would elaborate.

He nodded and again said that he was there for me and that he was innocent. I began to laugh like, yeah, right. We're all innocent.

"I'll only be here a short season because I'm here for you," he repeated.

The next day, while exercising, I looked across the way and saw the same guy bowed down across a blanket. I had never seen anything like it before, but it struck something deep within me. There he was, in his cell, completely bowed down.

I worked out, took a shower, made myself a spread. Oh, that's ramen noodle soup with chips, sausage, and cheese, but nearly two hours later, I looked over at him again, and he was still bowed down. When he finally got up, I ran to the gate and shouted, "Hey, what were you doing?"

"I was praying and asking God to show me what he had for you," he said.

Praying that long seemed very odd to me. All I knew about official prayers were repeating things like The Lord's Prayer and the Hail Mary. What did he mean he was asking God to show him something? How can you actually talk to God, I thought.

"Have you ever read the Bible?" he asked.

"No." I was ashamed, but really, who actually reads the Bible?

In reality, I think a lot of people have a Bible more for decoration, yet are ignorant of the Truth it holds. Without cracking it open and reading God's love letter written to them, they will never experience freedom of the knowledge of who God is.

"Read it," was his simple request.

I thought, sure, why not? It wasn't like I had anything else to do for the next four years. But still, the idea of me reading God's Word seemed weird. In the Catholic religion, the priest always read the Bible to us. Unfortunately, most of those readings were in Latin.

That night, I figured I'd try it out for myself. I opened that Bible and ended up staying up all night reading it. Something strange and wonderful was happening on the inside of me. I first opened it up to Proverbs, and immediately, it seemed as if a hand came up out of the pages and grabbed my face and pulled me in. It was incredible, so I inhaled Psalms, and eventually, the four Gospels: Matthew, Mark, Luke, and John.

At one point in my life, I felt that shooting meth was the best feeling ever. Well, God's Word was way better. It was so exhilarating. Although I only read what was required in school and the Navy, this was different because I wasn't only reading the Bible. The Bible was reading me.

The next day, I came out to the gate and yelled over to the pastor, "Guess what? I'm reading the Bible, and it's amazing!"

He grinned. "What'd you read about?"

"God," I chirped like a kid. "I read about God."

He stood silently, and I wondered if he was doubting me. Then he nodded and leaned toward me. I leaned back in.

"Read the Word like, hmmm, you know when you get your first commissary"—that's the store in prison—"and you get your first candy bar," he whispered. "And the way you lie back in your bunk and unwrap that Snickers bar, you eat it slowly and savor every bit. Think about, as you chew, how you get a picture of the crunchy peanuts and the sticky caramel chocolate. Make it last as long as you possibly can," he said. "Do you understand?"

"Yes," I sighed.

"That's how you read the Bible and spend time with God." He winked.

He wanted me to read the Bible slowly, so I would glean every bit of revelation I could from the Scriptures. In addition to reading the Bible, he told me to watch the same programs he did on TBN (Trinity Broadcasting Network). Here's where I was introduced to Creflo Dollar and Jesse Duplantis and Kenneth Copeland. I thought Jesse Duplantis was funny, and I wanted to become just like him. It got to the point where I actually yearned to hear him preach in person.

One day, I was made a trusty in the jail, and I realized that I had favor—just as Joseph did in Pharaoh's jail in Egypt. Looking back, I can see that I always had favor in whatever jail I was sent to. God's hand was on my life, and in these moments, I began gaining slices of His plan for my life. Because I'd been blessed with the chance to serve as a trusty, I wanted to repay the pastor as a way to show my appreciation. I grabbed extra sandwiches to take to him. I know it might sound trivial, but when you have nothing, even the smallest of things means something.

To my surprise, he was no longer there. He'd been freed because he had told the truth about his innocence. I laughed for a while because out of all the men I'd met in all my years behind bars, this was the one guy who was actually telling the truth. I never knew his name, but Ruthy believes he was an angel. Sometimes we take for granted those people in our lives who speak hard truth to us so that we don't fall for the lie. He impacted my life by telling me the truth. In a way, that prisoner on the other side of the cage was as much a father figure to me as anyone ever was.

A Man On Fire

And just like that, I started sharing God with everyone I spoke with. I couldn't stop talking about Him. We began holding Bible studies and prayer circles in the tank. I saw how some of the guys were growing in the things of God and how everything I did grew. Eventually, everywhere I went, there was a prayer circle. No matter where I would go or what I was doing, someone was going to hear about Jesus. I was truly a man on fire for Jesus.

Leadership speaker/author John Maxwell teaches that a leader knows the way, goes the way, and shows the way. Pastor Tom Lane of Gateway Church in Southlake, Texas, has stated, "The way we live our lives and serve the Lord determines the scope of our influence." I was learning that as Christians, we're called to be a people who refuse to compromise the truth. As we continue to live in the truth, we become truly free to lead others to that same freedom through Christ.

Miraculously, God did the impossible, and my sentence was reduced. He was turning my entire life around. For twenty-three years, my life was marked by stealing, killing, and destroying. Before, I couldn't care less who I hurt or what my future held. Now I could see clearly for the first time. I always thought everyone else had the problem, but it was me. In reality, I was lonely and depressed, looking for a quick fix and finding life in all the wrong places.

As I served out my time, Louisiana Baptist Seminary, as well as Exodus Prison Ministry, sent me stuff to study and pray and meditate over. I continued growing in my relationship with Jesus. I would get up at 4 a.m. to pray and study His Word. We started a faith-based pod in Mineral Wells, which no longer exists, but it was thriving back then. I had become a light in darkness. We had prayer circles outside by the tree on Saturdays, with a hundred or so men gathered for the services. God was stretching me beyond my comfort zone. He had a call on my life, and prison was the preparation ground He used to groom me for what was to come. Most of all, He gave me a new heart.

As the prophet Ezekiel wrote, "I [God] will give you a new heart and put a new spirit within you; I will take the heart of stone out of your flesh and give you a heart of flesh."

Back in the Land of Oz, it's time for the second character Dorothy encounters on the Yellow Brick Road to make his entrance: the Tin Man, who was in search of a heart.

6

THE RUSTY TIN MAN

THE LIE GOT YOU STUCK

The Tin Man is the next person Dorothy comes across on her journey into the city of Oz. Here we see that the Tin Man is "stuck" in life. Have you ever been stuck? Stuck in an abusive relationship? Stuck in an addiction or in some dead-end, never-changing, unproductive rut, something that keeps happening over and over again?

We call that a stronghold because it's like a prison for your soul, wrong thought patterns that prevent you from experiencing God's freedom and joy.

The Tin Man informs Dorothy that the first thing he needs to get unstuck is the oil can, and the first place the oil needs to be used is his mouth. If his mouth is oiled and loosened first, then he will be able to speak freely and let her know where the oil needs to be applied next.

The Bible has a lot to say about the power of the tongue and how our words affect us and others. The saying "sticks and stones may break my bones, but words will never hurt me" was a LIE: they could kill you! Oh, and "What I don't know won't hurt me." What you don't know could also kill you; people perish for lack of knowledge. Here are some scriptures that talk about the tongue:

The tongue of the righteous is choice silver, but the heart of the wicked is of little value.

Proverbs 10:20

From the mouth of the righteous comes the fruit of wisdom, but a perverse tongue will be silenced.

Proverbs 10:31

The words of the reckless pierce like swords, but the tongue of the wise brings healing.

Proverbs 12:18

The tongue of the wise adorns knowledge, but the mouth of the fool gushes folly.

Proverbs 15:2

The soothing tongue is a tree of life, but a perverse tongue crushes the spirit.

Proverbs 15:4

A wicked person listens to deceitful lips; a liar pays attention to a destructive tongue.

Proverbs 17:4

The tongue has the power of life and death, and those who love it will eat its fruit.

Proverbs 18:21

We all stumble in many ways. Anyone who is never at fault in what they say is perfect, able to keep their whole body in check. When we put bits into the mouths of horses to make them obey us, we can turn the whole animal. Or take ships as an example. Although they are so large and are driven by strong winds, they are steered by a very small rudder wherever the pilot wants to go. Likewise, the tongue is a small part of the body, but it makes great boasts. Consider what a great forest is set on fire by a small spark. The tongue also is a fire, a world of evil among the parts of the body. It corrupts the whole body, sets the whole course of one's life on fire, and is itself set on fire by hell...

No human being can tame the tongue. It is a restless evil, full of deadly poison. With the tongue, we praise our Lord and Father, and with it, we curse human beings, who have been made in God's likeness.

James 3:2-9 NIV

The first place the Tin Man needed the oil was his mouth so that he could get the rest of himself set free. Think about that! We are often snared and bound by our words, and it's probably the last place we think the anointing can transform our life.

Rather, we want the anointing applied to our music, so we sound great. Or we want it on our ministry so that people get healed when we pray for them. If we step back and take a close look at our lives, we'll see that our mouths are one of the primary places the anointing is needed and should be desired.

Listen to this account from the prophet Isaiah, who had an encounter with God that changed the course of his life:

"Woe to me!" I cried. "I am ruined! For I am a man of unclean lips, and I live among a people of unclean lips, and my eyes have seen the King, the Lord Almighty." Then one of the seraphim flew to me with a live coal in his hand, which he had taken with tongs from the altar. With it, he touched my mouth and said, "See, this has touched your lips; your guilt is taken away, and your sin atoned for."

Isaiah 6:5-7 NIV

In Isaiah's response, after God calls him to be a prophet, he cries out that he is a man of "unclean lips." As you journey further along the road that God has placed before you, leading to all the promises He has in store for you, you must demand that the anointing of God be placed on your lips.

The more time we spend with Jesus, the more the anointing becomes evident in our lives. And that's not all; the same anointing affecting us will also begin to affect those around us. This is another reason why it's good to realize there is power in our words. Did you ever imitate actors by saying the things they said in a movie, or go along singing the words to whatever songs you listened to? If you do this long enough, you will start to see those things you confess and declare come to fruition.

You may be wondering why I'm talking so much about the power of the tongue when this chapter is about the heart (remember, the Tin Man wanted a new heart). Here's your answer. One day, speaking from a hillside to a great crowd of people, Jesus said, "A good man brings good things out of the good stored up in his heart, and an evil man brings evil things out of the evil stored up in his heart. For the mouth speaks what the heart is full of" (Luke 6:45).

About a thousand years earlier, King Solomon also said,

"Above all else, guard your heart, for everything you do flows from it" (Proverbs 4:23).

The anointing of God does a work in your *heart* so that you can walk according to your confessions. Don't miss this! The words you speak affect your life.

Dorothy applies the oil to the Tin Man's mouth, then to his shoulders and elbows, because once our confession goes forth, we are meant to move in that direction. Likewise, our body needs to become subject to the Holy Spirit—that means living in purity.

Oftentimes, we say something like "my flesh made me do it," but that only means we are not yet surrendered to Christ. Our flesh has to become crucified because to die in the flesh is to gain in the Spirit. The apostle Paul struggled with the same dilemma of struggling in the flesh, yet he offers a solution:

[18] For I know that nothing good lives within the flesh of my fallen humanity. The longings to do what is right are within me, but will-power is not enough to accomplish it.

[19] My lofty desires to do what is good are dashed when I do the things I want to avoid. [20] So if my behavior contradicts my desires to do good, I must conclude that it's not my true identity doing it, but the unwelcome intruder of sin *hindering me from being who I really am.*

[21] Through my experience of this principle, I discover that even when I want to do good, evil is ready to sabotage me. [22] Truly, deep within my true identity, I love to do what pleases God.

[23] But I discern another power operating in my humanity, waging a war against the moral principles of my conscience and bringing me into captivity as a prisoner to the "law" of sin—this unwelcome intruder in my humanity.

[24] What an agonizing situation I am in! So who has the power to rescue this miserable man from the unwelcome intruder of sin and death?

[25] I give all my thanks to God, for his mighty power has finally provided a way out through our Lord Jesus, the Anointed One! So if left to myself, the flesh is aligned with the law of sin, but now my renewed mind is fixed on and submitted to God's righteous principles.

Romans 7:18-25 TPT

Follow Your Confession

We spend way too much time using the excuse "well, I'm not perfect" or "I'm only human" when really, your flesh will follow your confession, which comes from your heart. Yes, we will experience setbacks, but there should always be a greater comeback. We should always be growing. Think about it: what if you saw one of your thirty-year-old friends in a shopping cart? Exactly: we should be maturing in the things of Christ.

The storm in Dorothy's life took her to a place where she could do an honest assessment of who she was on the inside. We should be saying, *search me oh God, and know my heart...*

With each person she met along the journey, she felt as though she had known them her whole life. As the movie unfolds, through a spiritual lens, we realize that the place Dorothy journeyed to was a destination she could always reach because she now had access through a changed heart and a renewed way of thinking.

As she related to each of the characters, she was able to get back into step with truth and continue her journey down the Yellow Brick Road. The strongholds in Dorothy's life needed to be broken so that she might then bring them into alignment with her life's truth and freedom. God wants to do the same with you, and again, He's asking you the question: Will you follow me along heaven's Yellow Brick Road?

First John 1:5-9 says:

...God is light; in him, there is no darkness at all. If we claim to have fellowship with him and yet walk in the darkness, we lie and do not live out the truth. [7] But if we walk in the light, as he is in the light, we have fellowship with one another, and the blood of Jesus, his Son, purifies us from all sin. If we claim to be without sin, we deceive ourselves, and the truth is not in us. If we confess our sins, he is faithful and just and will forgive us our sins and purify us from all unrighteousness.

We see Dorothy's life coming into alignment as she becomes in sync with each of the other characters, one by one, as they all follow the Yellow Brick Road. Before we are able to move along the Yellow Brick Road, we do have to get in sync with God's will. Repenting is a big part of that spiritual alignment. Pastor Bill Johnson of Bethel Church in Redding, California, once broke down the word *repentance* this way: "pent," meaning the top floor, and that to repent is to get to the top way of thinking, which is God's way. As we see Dorothy getting in step with the Scarecrow and the Tin Man, we see the beginning of her taking her path and life to a clearer, purposeful, and a higher way of thinking and being.

To walk a victorious Christian life, we need to expose the lie of the enemy—those seductive words he whispers in our ear to get us off track and lure us into temptation. It was really never about my addictive behaviors; those were the fruit of my rooted issues.

Dr. Michael Dye, in *The Genesis Process* book, talks about belief systems. For instance, having confidence in something you think is true but is actually a lie is a false belief system. If you have a belief system that is true and reality bears witness to that truth, then you have a true belief system.

True beliefs are based on the Word of God; false beliefs are based on fear or arise out of loss or pain. True beliefs increase value and growth in your life; false beliefs demean and diminish the value and growth of your life. True beliefs edify both self and others, while false beliefs are proven false by destructive defensive behaviors. True beliefs create peace and confidence, while false beliefs create anxiety and exhaustion.

I'm hoping you get the concept. It's time for you to expose the lie and accept the truth that brings love, joy, peace, patience, kindness, goodness, faithfulness, gentleness, and self-control. All the things that only the spirit of God can give you and me.

I'm here to tell you, with the help of the Holy Spirit, you can cut fellowship with the old way of thinking. The light of Christ brings alignment with the Truth, and repentance opens you up to a higher level of thinking. With your new heart and your renewed mind, you truly are a *new creation*.

> Therefore if any man be in Christ, he is a new creature: old things are passed away; behold, all things are become new.
> 2 Corinthians 5:17 KJV

Coming into alignment with God's Truth is like this: imagine a car that's been driven over potholes and bad roads for a long time. Eventually, that car pulls hard to the left or right, and you need to take it in for a wheel alignment so the mechanic can center it and stop the pull. We too need constant life alignments to stay the course.

And, most of all, we need courage to face what God has called us to do.

7

I HAVE A LION INSIDE OF ME
FINDING THE COURAGE TO ADVANCE

As Dorothy, the Scarecrow, and the Tin Man travel along the path, they encounter the next addition to their party: the Lion. The Lion jumps out of the woods, roaring to intimidate them. The Lion even gets to the point of scaring poor little Toto, chasing him around. Funny that he comes out as a roaring lion, looking to see who he can devour. At first, he has them all scared. However, the moment Dorothy confronts the fear and abuse, she is able to obtain "Courage."

In our walk with Jesus, we have the revelation of the cross and the blood of Jesus, which knocked out the enemy's teeth. Just as Dorothy comes out and binds the strong man, so must we. She slaps the lion and commands him to stop picking on people. Prior to Dorothy's arrival, he was always picking on weak people, and Dorothy puts an end to it.

In high school, there was this guy I would always pick on by calling him names. I see now that the enemy used me to lie to someone about who they were in an attempt to destroy their identity. Sadly, a lot of parents do this without even knowing it. Parents call their children "stupid," "good for nothing," along with all sorts of terrible names that demean their identity.

Name-calling attaches labels and false identities to people that God would never ascribe to them; *The Genesis Process* calls those projected lies. When other people talk to you, they take their own hurts and fears and project them onto you, then that creates survival lies, which are the lies people tell themselves as a way to survive.

Going a little deeper, names mean something in the spiritual realm. Every time I saw this person in high school, I would call him something very degrading. Yes, I was a bully for a season in my life.

One day during lunch, I was hanging outside a store and noticed that this same young man was on his way in. As he walked into the store, I started calling him names, and I continued mocking him in front of everyone all through the store; even as he was coming out, I continued to make fun as all the others laughed. As he took a few steps out the door, he spun around and hit me right in the mouth. BOOM! Now, at that time, I wore braces, and blood spurted everywhere. Let me tell you, after that day, I thought twice about mocking that guy or anyone ever again (LOL).

In hindsight, the Lord revealed to me something about that day. It was a revelation on how to defeat the enemy. It's true! You have to bind the strongman. When you bind the enemy, you shut him up. This guy was tired of my calling him names, and he put me in my place. No, you can't physically punch the devil, but you sure can war against him in your prayer closet.

We punch the devil by acknowledging the lie, exposing it as a lie, and then replacing it with the truth of God. Jesus defeated the enemy with one simple quote: "It is written."

As long as the bully can bully you, he will demand a dollar a day. If he's not confronted, he will start to demand two dollars a day, then five. Believe me, he will continue to push his limits to what you allow. That's exactly what happened with this young man and me. After that fight, I stopped calling him names.

The enemy will roam around looking for weak people who won't put up a fight. If we are vulnerable, weak, and open, the enemy will come in and take over. Not knowing who you are, where you are from, or being ignorant about your legal rights spiritually will leave you vulnerable, weak, and open to the enemy's mayhem. He will be the one binding you and plundering your house instead of you shutting him down like you ought to.

One day, I was preaching on Philippians 3:20—which talks about us being citizens of heaven—during a time when our nation was experiencing a great racial divide, and I remember saying, "We aren't JamaiCAN, Puerto RiCAN, AfriCAN, or even MexiCAN...we are HeaviCANs because we are citizens of heaven."

The word *Heavican* has since become a powerful statement for me because it unifies us all and lets us know our identity is in nothing earthly but in Christ and all things kingdom. If we were in France and I were a US ambassador, I would have an embassy I could go to for safety.

When I was growing up in New York, I would see these special diplomatic license plates. I used to get so upset because they could always park in places that I couldn't, and I never understood why they never got a ticket. The reason is because they were operating out of the legalities of the nation they represented. In other words, they had diplomatic immunity.

Likewise, if I were an ambassador for America, no matter where I went, it would be the same for me as if I were on American soil. This is the same for us as citizens of heaven! I'm an ambassador of heaven, living here on the earth, and I have full authority to operate in and release the kingdom of heaven here on earth.

Deputized By Heaven

When I think about a new heart, a new mind, and the boldness of the Lion of Judah, I feel like I'm one with God. When you possess these things, there's nothing missing, nothing broken, and you have a complete *sozo* (inner healing) experience with God. You realize that you are saved and sanctified in every way by His word.

There's something undeniable about the call of God on your life. When He apprehends you and sets your feet on a new course, your whole life is charged with new meaning and purpose.

Even if, like the Lion on the Yellow Brick Road, you feel less than courageous before God apprehends you, suddenly you are infused with a zeal that can only come from the Holy Spirit. You might be nervous or afraid, but because you trust in God and are led by His spirit, you move forward.

One way to describe it is to say you are now deputized by heaven to perform whatever God has called you to do. For me, it was to go back to sow life and purpose in the very town where I had sown death and destruction for so many years. For a man named Gideon, being deputized by heaven meant leading an army against a brutal enemy.

We first meet Gideon as he is threshing wheat in a winepress to hide it from the Midianites. This nation had tormented Israel for seven years, destroying their crops and killing their livestock. When the people of Israel cried out to God for help, He answered by sending the angel of the Lord to visit Gideon.

The angel sits down under an oak tree and says, "The Lord is with you, mighty warrior." The King James translation says, "Thou mighty man of valour."

So we see that the angel's first words *call forth* what God saw in Gideon, not what Gideon thought of himself. He was just threshing wheat—and hiding, at that, so the enemy wouldn't confiscate the grain.

Gideon struggles to believe that God has actually visited him and puts the angel through a series of three miraculous "proofs" before he's on board. And what does God want him to do? Lead an army of Israel's warriors against the Midianites and conquer them!

Uh, can you repeat that, God? That's what most of us would be thinking, but Gideon rises to the challenge. Newly deputized by heaven, he assembles an army of thirty-two thousand men and prepares to attack the Midianites.

God, however, tells Gideon that the army is too great in number; with that many men, Israel will boast that they won the victory in their own strength.

So God commands Gideon to whittle the army down, letting any men who prefer to return home to do so; twenty-two thousand take the offer, leaving ten thousand behind. That's still too many, God says—

and devises another means to reduce the number of warriors down to just three hundred.

If you've read the story in the Bible, you know what happens. The Israelites sneak into the camp of Midian at night, carrying only shofars (trumpets) and clay jars with a torch hidden inside.

At Gideon's signal, all the men blow their shofars, give a battle cry, and light their torches, simulating the attack of a very large army. The Midianites flee in confusion and terror, Israel pursues and kills them, then captures their princes and claims the victory.

Here's what I want you to see in this story. When the angel of the Lord first calls Gideon, he makes excuses for why he's not up to the task.

> The Lord turned to him and said, "Go in the strength you have and save Israel out of Midian's hand. Am I not sending you?"
>
> ¹⁵ "Pardon me, my lord," Gideon replied, "but how can I save Israel? My clan is the weakest in Manasseh, and I am the least in my family."
>
> ¹⁶ The Lord answered, "I will be with you, and you will strike down all the Midianites, leaving none alive."
>
> Judges 6:14-16 NIV

But twenty verses later, in verse 34, something has happened to Gideon. He is a new man, full of zeal and courage. Look what the Scripture says:

Then the **Spirit of the Lord** came on Gideon, and he blew a trumpet, summoning the [men] to follow him.

Ah, did you catch it? *The Spirit of the Lord came on Gideon...*

We may feel unworthy, insignificant, or even cowardly like the Lion Dorothy meets on the Yellow Brick Road, but once God gets ahold of us and commissions us with His purpose, we are forever changed as long as we "hold fast to our confession" and keep moving forward.

Leader Before, Leader After

Have you ever noticed how God assigned the "heroes of faith" in the Bible to tasks they had already trained for in their past?

- Jacob's tenacity led him to wrestle with the angel of the Lord all night and not let go until God blessed him; he became the father of the twelve tribes of Israel (his new name).
- Joseph, an arrogant youth, dreamed that his family would one day bow down to him; even though God took Joseph through thirteen years of shaping and humbling, he stayed faithful—and eventually became the prime minister of Egypt. God used another dream to give Joseph wisdom on how to save his family and the whole region from starvation during a famine.
- Moses was plucked from the Nile River as a baby, trained to be a prince of Egypt, but identified with his own people, the Hebrews, who were enslaved by the Egyptians; he ran away from Egypt and spent years herding sheep in the desert until God sent him back to deliver His people and "shepherd" them.
- David tended sheep, killed lions and bears, then one day killed a giant who blasphemed the name of the Lord; God anointed David as king so he could shepherd the people of Israel.
- Luke, a trained doctor who was used to taking meticulous notes, later penned the longest Gospel in the canon of Scripture.
- Paul, formerly Saul, took a leadership role in stamping out followers of The Way until God apprehended him on the Damascus Road; he became the chief apostle to the gentiles and wrote most of the New Testament.

I look over my own life now and marvel how God took a drug

dealer who was prideful, insecure, lustful, angry, and lost—someone who could come into an area and quickly take it over, a mover and shaker in Satan's kingdom— and now has made me the man I am today.

Every day, I feel like I'm dreaming, except for dreams, you have to be asleep, and I am fully awake. The great things about the promises of God is that He completely restores your life. While being incarcerated in Weatherford, Texas, might've started off as a nightmare, I'd soon come to be blessed with the family God had always intended for me.

8

HISPANIC BRADY BUNCH

THE PROCESS TO THE PROMISE

One day while sitting on my bunk, I looked up and gazed right into the eyes of a young man I'd never seen before. When I say young, I mean it. This kid was all of nineteen years old and already behind bars. I asked his name, and he said Johnathan.

I was no longer surprised when God surprised me, and this time, it took the form of a strange new love: the heart of a father. Looking at this kid, I felt compassionate and protective of him. Funny, because I also had a son named Johnathan. I never really got to see him, and I felt as though God were saying to me, "Here is your son."

With this, I made the decision to love him as I would my own son. I began discipling him, and he would join me in the prayer circles. We prayed together over many different things, one of them being his mom, Ruthy. I remember praying she would find a church, and later, Johnathan would come back all excited saying that she found one. And so I was praying and believing for Ruthy often.

One day, I decided to write Ruthy to tell her all about how her son was doing. At first, she didn't care to write me back, probably thinking I was some crazy convict—and I don't blame her. But eventually, God put it in her heart to write me back. She told me she was going to Houston Worship Centre and that her pastor, Randy Needham, was preaching the same messages that I was writing to her about in my letters.

This went on for months, and she was kind of in shock how that could be happening. I didn't know Pastor Randy, so it was like confirmation that we were supposed to be writing. God was also speaking into her life and guiding her into truth. She finally realized that it was from God, and I was cleared of being some crazy convict. This story doesn't end here, and maybe I'll share more later or have to write another book (LOL) of our amazing love story.

Walking The Line

In the prison yard, they had painted these yellow lines that we were supposed to walk on for exercise. There were almost two thousand men, and no one really walked the lines. One day, the Lord said to me, "You need to walk the line." Because of my love for Him, I started to follow the rules. People would yell at me, "Hey, New York! What are you doing over there?" I was the only guy walking the line, while everyone else was all over the place.

I was the only guy! Do you understand what I'm saying?

I remember being embarrassed about it, and when people asked me what I was doing, I didn't want to tell them it was because God told me to do it. I was still in my pride, but I walked the line regardless. While walking the lines, God would talk to me about walking the narrow road. He shared with me that if I couldn't change my life in the little things, I would never do it in the big things. If I was going to stay out of prison, I would have to change in the little ways. God showed me a picture of the world and how broad the path is that leads to destruction. The world didn't want to walk the line, but I was called to, in hope that others would eventually follow the narrow path too.

I even started to walk the yellow lines to church. When the other church guys asked me why I was walking the line, I said it was because God told me to. Before long, three would follow me. Then there were five, which grew to ten or twenty people depending on the day.

Now remember, there were two thousand people in that prison

yard. God says that only a few will follow the narrow path, and I was grateful to be numbered among the few that did. After some time, at the end of the line, I would try to take a two-foot shortcut.

One day, the Lord asked me why I couldn't adhere to the line all the way to the end. He asked me why I decided to take the shortcut. My response was nonchalant. I didn't think it was that big a deal, and He said something that has stayed with me till today.

He said, "In life, there are no shortcuts. You either follow Me all the way through or you don't." This rocked my world, so I explained it to the others, but they still chose to take the shortcut. The Bible says, "Those who are led by the Spirit of God are sons of God" (Romans 8:14). See, we often think that the shortcut is faster, but it's really the longcut that's the shortcut (lol). Let me explain: in the shortcut, it eventually messes up because you face a battle you weren't ready for, and what could have taken you a year now takes three years or sometimes longer because we don't allow the process to take place. If you walk it out and allow the process to do what it's supposed to do, then the longcut only gets done one time, and you're done and on to the next. We see this example in

Exodus 13:17-18 CSB

[17] When Pharaoh let the people go, God did not lead them along the road to the land of the Philistines, even though it was nearby; for God said, "The people will change their minds and return to Egypt if they face war."[18] So he led the people around toward the Red Sea along the road of the wilderness. And the Israelites left the land of Egypt in battle formation.

Allow God's process to take you into His promise. He knew that if they went into something prematurely, they would lose and get discouraged, and that would cause them to return to Egypt. We often behave like the newly freed Israelites because we don't hesitate to run back to the things in our past that once held us captive.

Okay, let's get back to my process.

The faith-based pod we started was made up of about ninety men, and we held our meetings on the third floor—the same floor the men would go to if they wanted to smoke; it was also where they would meet up to fight. However, during our meeting time, I announced that none of that would be happening while we were there.

Although I was a bit nervous, I knew God's spirit was leading me and I would be okay. Eventually, I gained respect and favor from almost everybody. I even had gang members stand up for me, telling people they better leave me alone. Talk about favor!

A Testing Of Faith

The day before I got out, the guards did a shakedown and went through everything on our floor. To accomplish this, they would send us packing from one side of the prison to the other. This meant I had to carry two sacks of books, a mattress, and my clothes. It was a long walk, and everything seemed so heavy. I ended up dropping all my stuff, and other guys were trying to help me, all while the guards kept yelling, "Let him carry it all himself." At once, my thoughts turned to Jesus and the weight of the cross He had to carry. What a moment of revelation. He has gone before me and can sympathize with everything I am going through. The very next day, I was released.

At the moment of becoming a free man, my faith was tested immediately. Upon being released, I was given $50 cash as part of the State of Texas's contribution for getting back on my feet. Then I was asked a question: "Do you want to buy any cigarettes?" My very first decision as a free man was whether to buy cigarettes or not. Although the urge was strong, I decided to say no, and I went about my way.

I'd quit smoking while in prison because I didn't want to be a prisoner to any substance or addiction. While still on the inside, I was able to resist the temptation, but once I arrived at the Greyhound station, everybody around me was smoking. It seemed that no matter where I turned, there it was right in my face. In this moment of feeling weak and surrounded by temptation, I remembered a man named Mike Lanier. Mike was part of a prison ministry, and he gave me his personal number for me to reach out when I was in need, and so I did.

The minute you give in to temptation, you compromise the truth. Even the smallest of temptations can drag you right back into prison. Think of it this way: every time you say no to a temptation, you say yes to a promise. God says He will give us the desires of our heart if we will take delight in Him. The problem is we usually pet the thing that could destroy us. Example: a tiger cub that looks cute and you keep petting it, feeding it, and aw, how cute, but eventually, it grows up and eats you alive. That's what we do with temptation: we pet it daily like it's no big deal, and when you least expect it, you have a ravenous tiger in your face.

When I got out of prison, Ruthy asked me if I had plans to move to Houston. Even though I wanted to be near her, for the first time in my life, I realized that I needed to get myself in a good place before I could be in a good place for someone else. With that, I decided to go to Calvary Commission in Lyndale, Texas, with Pastor Joe Foss. The time I spent there was amazing and much needed. I spent most of my time studying His Word, and I was able to learn how to integrate back into society, all the while holding true to the Word that was being written on the inside of me.

From Dope Dealer To Love Healer

After Calvary Commission, I did move to Houston and began to build my life back. At this time, Ruthy and I were just friends, and even though I did have a growing interest, I had absolutely no money to help her with a single thing. I didn't even have enough money to buy her a glass of iced tea. Besides that, my clothes were all too big, and I had a big hole on the bottom of my left shoe. Ruthy stuck by my side anyway and decided to believe with me.

We attended church together at Houston Worship Centre, and I developed this overwhelming passion for ministry. I often asked her if she wanted to go with me back to the old towns where I once sowed death so that I could now sow life. Instead of returning as a dope dealer, I was on a mission to reveal Jesus and my new life as a Love dealer, and I was giving it away for free.

One day in a small group breakout session, I was sharing my heart toward the people whose lives I destroyed, and I knew it was time for me to go back. Right then and there, we stood in agreement with God's plan for ministry through my life, and Ruthy and my friend Amber joined me on my first mission trip back to Breckenridge, Texas.

Without knowing what we were doing or how we should do it, we boldly went from door to door, wrapping people in the love of Christ. A few people even thought it was a trap. I'm sure for them to see me outside their door was a little scary. However, God moved in the hearts of the people we visited, and to my surprise, their hearts would break for God, and many were healed and set free from addiction.

It was truly amazing to see God's plan for my life in ministry unfold right before my eyes. Soon after our first trip, God opened doors for me to share my testimony at a few churches in Breckenridge. The services would be packed with people who formerly knew me as New York J. They couldn't believe their eyes or their ears, but they saw something real, and they wanted to know more. By the end of service, the altars would be packed.

One evening, after sharing with a congregation, I felt led to pass the offering plate back around. This time it wasn't for a monetary offering. I told the congregation that God wanted to deliver some people, but they had to offer up what they'd been holding on to in their pockets. When we received the offering plate back, it was full of blunts, meth, and even needles. We were shocked to see how powerfully God was moving and that the people of Breckenridge were ripe for the taking.

Even with the ministry taking off as quickly as it did, I swallowed my pride and enrolled in a school of ministry at All Nations School of Revival. During my time in All Nations, I shared testimonies of what God was doing in Breckenridge, and several people wanted in. We started a "Love Breckenridge" campaign and assembled outreach teams. The first outreach was held at a park, and about one thousand people came out.

From there, we began to visit on a regular basis. We formed different teams and went from house to house and church to church, allowing God to use us in whatever way He saw fit. God kept doing what only He could do: save, heal, and set free.

I would have to write another book just to contain all the testimonies of what God did in the small town of Breckenridge. However, the one thing that I must share is the way that God moved to unite the hearts of pastors, priests, and people alike. It was beautiful to see people of faith erase the man-made boundary lines of denominationalism for the sake of serving others. We truly moved as the singular, Holy Spirit-filled Body of Christ.

In John 17, Jesus prays the most moving prayer you'll ever read. He was praying for His twelve disciples, but He was also praying for us—those who would believe in Him two centuries later.

> Now I am no longer in the world, but these are in the world, and I come to You. Holy Father, keep through Your name those whom You have given Me, that they may be one as We are.
>   John 17:11-12 NIV

During our early days of ministry, we saw this scripture being fulfilled before our eyes. God is so good.

God Plays Matchmaker

Not too long after we started ministering together, I knew in my heart that I wanted to marry Ruthy. As I pursued her, I really surprised myself. Now I knew that I was truly a changed man, seeing that my heart wanted to wait until marriage to have sex. It was the first time in my life that I had a healthy and God-honoring relationship. We did things the right way, and it was a huge victory for both of us. What a fairy tale, right? I got to marry the Ruthy I was writing to in prison— the mother of Johnathan, whom God had brought alongside me to disciple and love as my own son.

Today we are like the Hispanic Brady Bunch. Together, we have six children. In the first few years of ministry, one by one, our children were reconciled to us, and only God can get the glory from that story.

He truly is faithful, if only we will put our trust in Him and Him alone.

After we married, the ministry took off even more. Doors opened for us as evangelists. God sparked fires all over, through our testimony and His Word that was etched on our hearts. We have planted churches in the north and southside of Houston; we also have a campus in New London, Connecticut, and a Spanish congregation called That's Crazy, No That's God. We had been called, commissioned, and sent forth. Now it was up to us to stay the course.

9

FOLLOW THE YELLOW BRICK ROAD

STAYING THE COURSE

When Dorothy asks about how to get to the city of Oz, she is told to simply start at the beginning, aka Genesis. The message God is giving me as I write this book is to go back to His original plan—be fruitful and multiply. We complicate things that God has made so simple. His call on your life and my life is the same one He gave to Adam in the Garden: be fruitful and multiply.

Jesus informed His twelve disciples that He was making them fishers of men. He spoke of fields white unto harvest, representing souls ready to be brought into the kingdom. He told parables about people using what God had given them and yielding a return. He also let us know we would have troubles—storms—in this world, but told us to be of good cheer, because He has overcome the world.

At the end of Dorothy's journey through the land of Oz, and even after meeting the Wizard, her perspective changes. It wasn't that she needed to become a whole other Dorothy; it had more to do with her becoming the best version of herself. Going through a trial won't make you a whole other person, but it will challenge you to become the best version of "you" who God created you to be.

Dorothy's storm helped reconcile her family, and she was able to see what she had been given in life was a blessing. She also came to realize that everything she ever needed in life was already there. God will often use the people in your life to show you what you need to see and to tell you what you need to hear. Throughout the Gospels, Jesus says, "He who has eyes to see, let him see, and he who has ears to hear, let him hear."

Paved With The Word

If Dorothy had strayed from the Yellow Brick Road, her journey would have led to a lot of unnecessary frustration and confusion. However, Dorothy stayed the course of following the Yellow Brick Road. In the same way that our prayers lay out before us the path on which we should go, we also must choose to stay that course.

My brothers and sisters, please understand this: if we want to fulfill our purpose in God—if we want to see His will accomplished in our life—there is no other road to take than the one established by prayer and paved, brick by brick, by the Word of God. Proverbs 14:12 says, "There is a path before each person that seems right, but it ends in death." While we are on the righteous path, "Flying Monkeys" will always try to take us off-course—things like habits and addictions, greed and lust, bad choices, and unwholesome company. We must be careful what we choose.

Check out this passage from James 1:19-20:

My dear brothers and sisters, take note of this. Everyone should be quick to listen, slow to speak, and slow to become angry, for a man's anger does not bring about the righteous life that God desires.

Did you get that? We must be *quick* to listen to God to what He has to say. He also knew you would want to answer back, so He says shut up (lol), to be slow to speak and *slow* to anger because He knew we would get angry. He's a loving father and knows best. At times, you will have to face yourself in the mirror of God's Word, and you won't like what it says. I can tell when people want to hang on to certain things God is calling them to give up because they act like a baby who doesn't want his toy taken away. I call that King baby syndrome.

It's amazing to see grown men get upset and try to justify their sin, and it's obvious they don't want to give it up. For those who do want change, learn to be slow to speak, because when the Word reveals something to us, it's to bring about transformation. Oftentimes, our quick response is a sign of us wanting to stay the way we are. We need to allow the Word to speak and move in our lives instead of being quick with an excuse or trying to justify why we are the way we are and do the things we do.

> Therefore, get rid of all moral filth and the evil that is so prevalent and humbly accept the Word planted in you, which can save you. Do not merely listen to the Word, and so deceive yourselves. Do what it says. Anyone who listens to the Word but does not do what it says is like a man who looks at his face in a mirror and, after looking at himself, goes away and immediately forgets what he looks like.
>   James 1: 21-24 NIV

It's funny how James chose to use a man in this example rather than a woman. When I'm getting ready to go somewhere, I'll look in the mirror once. I'll fix my hair, brush my teeth, and shave, all in that one look. After that, I don't bother looking in the mirror again. Ruthy, however, is very different. She will be in front of the mirror for a while, putting on makeup while she's worshipping Jesus and talking to me as I head out the door. After she's done with the bathroom mirror, she moves over in front of the tall mirror to see how everything looks from head to toe. You would think that would be enough, but then she'll get into the car and pull down the visor mirror to do some spot-checking. Boom, she closes that mirror and drives off to church. Then at church, she'll pull out a compact mirror for a close-up look to reapply lipstick. After saying hi to a few people, I guarantee she'll head to the bathroom to check once again in mirror number five.

Now, do you think she can forget what she looks like? I believe we need to start looking in the mirror like women do. The mirror I'm referring to is the Word, of course, but in the same way Ruthy looks obsessively, we need to be the same. We must look into the Word constantly so that we never forget what it says we look like. We also need to believe that the reflection the Word shows us of ourselves is true, and we must continually allow for it to bring about transformation. Remember, a mirror can't comb your hair. It can only show you it's messy and you must comb it. In this case, it's up to us to follow Jesus and His lead according to what the mirror is showing you.

One time, Ruthy and I were having a relaxation day at a resort here in The Woodlands. For hours, we decided to float around this "lazy river." We had no suntan lotion, no sunscreen, no nothing. Later that day, I realized I was sunburned. I wasn't tan or a little red; I was burned. The next day, as I looked at myself in the mirror, my skin started to peel off. Right then, God decided to use that as a teaching moment. He said to me, "When you spend time in the Sun-Son, the flesh falls."

For you to get where God wants to take you, you must stay on the path and remain consistent. If we believe that God orders our steps, then we need a continuous download of who we are, who God is, and what it is that He's asking us to do. Due to the Fall, we are in constant need of updates, and prayer is that continual communication with God that maintains the much-needed updates in our lives—the same way our phones constantly have new updates available for download to fix problems that come up.

Consider this nautical analogy by a pastor about the importance of staying on course:

If you've ever done any boating, you know how essential it is to stay on course. If you steer just a few degrees off the desired course, you can wind up far from where you wanted to go. I read once of a shipwreck that happened because a sailor broke off the small tip of his knife blade while he was cleaning the ship's compass. He didn't remove it, and that little bit of metal pulled the compass off its true reading, resulting in the ship's running aground. A slight deviation, if left uncorrected, can result in great devastation.

It's the same spiritually. Correction is not a nicety; it's a necessity. If our lives veer off-course and continue in that wrong direction, it can result in a shipwreck of our faith.

Stay Connected To The Source

This reminds me of a time when we had our Get Wrapped church van. We had just put new tires on it, changed the oil, and made sure everything was in working order. Then one day, it wouldn't start, and we couldn't figure out why. After a closer inspection, I noticed that corrosion had built up on the battery posts, so I cleaned the posts, reattached the cables, and the van started up just fine. There was really nothing wrong with the van, only that little bit of corrosion was interfering with a much-needed connection to the battery. Much like when Dorothy gets to Oz, and a much-needed connection is made.

> His divine power has given us everything we need for a life and godliness through our knowledge of Him who called us by His own glory and goodness. Through these, He has given us His very great and precious promises, so that through them, you may participate in the divine nature and escape the corruption in the world caused by evil desires. For this very reason, we make every effort...
> 2 Peter 1:3-5 NIV

Here we see that God has given us everything we need for a life filled with godliness. We are lacking nothing because everything we need has already been given to us. Now, the fifth verse tells us that we need to "make every effort." That means the ball is in our court, and we have a big part to play in this. God has given us everything we need, but He isn't going to do everything for us. He is just the mirror, remember?

What does Peter instruct us to "make every effort" in?

> ...add to your faith goodness; and to goodness, knowledge; and to knowledge, self-control; and to self-control, perseverance; and to perseverance, godliness; and to godliness, mutual affection; and to mutual affection, love. For if you possess these qualities in increasing measure, they will keep you from being ineffective and unproductive in your knowledge of our Lord Jesus Christ. But

whoever does not have them is nearsighted and blind, forgetting that they have been cleansed from their past sins.

2 Peter 1:5b-9 NIV

Think about a person who is overweight. They have a treadmill they don't use, but it's not because the machine doesn't work; it's because the treadmill is not being applied. Making every effort means to use everything God has provided to its fullest potential. We have to be intentional to withdraw what grace has already placed there for us.

Peter doesn't pull any punches; he finishes his admonition above with this:

Therefore, my brothers and sisters, make every effort to confirm your calling and election. For if you do these things, you will never stumble, and you will receive a rich welcome into the eternal kingdom of our Lord and Savior Jesus Christ.

2 Peter 1:10-11 NIV

Effort is not a popular word in today's culture. We want everything the easy way, the instant way, but God is all about forming us into the image of His Son, Jesus Christ—and that takes time. Salvation happens in a moment, but sanctification through his word is a lifelong process.

If you stay the course, Peter is telling us, if you "make every effort to confirm your calling and election," you will make it.

There's a reason why God has not made our journey down the Yellow Brick Road too easy. That's the subject of our next chapter.

10

BEWARE THE POPPY FIELD
THE DANGER OF TRANQUILITY'S TRAP

As the Yellow Brick Road leads them out of the forest, Dorothy and her new friends finally see the highly anticipated Emerald City, shining in all its glory, just beyond a beautiful field of green grass and wildflowers. Finally, they are "out of the woods," but only literally speaking. Figuratively, we discover they are still very much in the fight, except this fight is deceptive. Let's enter into the poppy field too, alongside our friends.

We must beware of the poppy field. Why, you ask? Why should we be concerned now that we see beauty as far as the eye can see? After all, we just came out of a scary forest ridden with uncertainty. The poppy field may seem like a place that's full of peace and calm, but if you are not careful, you might relax, thinking that the war is over.

We all go through the poppy fields along our journey as Christ-followers. The poppy field is a place you will find yourself in while praying through situations, and it may feel as though you can finally breathe, but be careful not to take a break completely—not just yet. Consider this: you finally get past the trials in the woods, and now the Emerald City is within plain sight, so naturally, you feel the temptation to stop and relax. This temptation is a strong one too! Stronger than the temptation you had to give up when things seemed impossible.

If we are not careful to understand what happens next, we will give in to the temptation to take a break and end up falling short of our goal. Often, the break we take lasts way longer than we ever intended it to. We might find ourselves lazily situated in a field of complacency. All the while, the goal is right in front of you, yet you choose to stay in this place of comfort and peace. This is where your resolve to reach your goal is tested the most. There will be times when you must resist the urge to choose comfort. You will need to stay focused, with your eyes on the promise. We must choose to persevere until we get there.

Answering The Call

What if Abraham wasn't the first person in his family to be called by God to go into Canaan, the Promised Land? If you choose to stay in that place of comfort between the fight and reaching the promise, and you find yourself stuck in the poppy field, you set up situations where other people will have to carry out what you were meant to accomplish.

> Terah took his son Abram, his grandson Lot son of Haran, and his daughter-in-law Sarai, the wife of his son Abram, and together they set out from Ur of the Chaldeans to go to Canaan. But when they came to Harran, they settled there.
> Genesis 11:31 NIV

Did you ever notice that the call was first placed on Abram's dad? Most of us only know that God told Abram to go to the land God would show him. Yet, the truth is, Terah was supposed to have already taken them there. God used Abram to continue the call that Abram's father fell short of completing. What do you imagine happened? Could it be that Terah decided to stop in a place that was comfortable and easy? Did he linger too long in a poppy field?

If we take an honest assessment, we often confuse the "rest of God" with the reality of complacency. God will never call us to be complacent. What's more, the Bible has nothing good to say about someone who chooses to be complacent.

> For the turning away of the simple will slay them, and the complacency of fools will destroy them.
> Proverbs 1:32 NKJV

Complacency is destructive because it lures us into thinking that we are in a safe place. Beyond that, it also causes us to believe that we can easily jump back on the journey, picking up in the same pace as before, whenever we finally decide to. Most often, this is not the case at all. Comfort leads to complacency, which leads us to our own casualty. What if Israel had decided to pitch a tent in the middle of the Red Sea? Pastor and evangelist Samuel Rodriguez says, "Today's complacency is tomorrow's captivity."

If the kingdom of God is always advancing, then complacency is super-destructive because it means the ground that should be taken isn't. As we see over and over in Scripture when one generation doesn't possess the territory God commanded them to take, the next generation is forced to battle for something that should have already been theirs, and overall progress is hindered.

The process of change is uncomfortable, but God brings comfort.

Israel dealt with this after coming out of Egypt before going into the land of Canaan. In their case, they were stuck in the wilderness for forty years. Forty years! All because they chose not to believe God, the very same God who brought them out of the storms of Pharaoh.

God wanted to take them into the Promised Land, even when they were too frightened because it appeared to be overrun with giants. We touched briefly on this story earlier, but let's go more in-depth here.

A Person Of A Different Spirit

If you look at this story the wrong way, it's easy to think God was being rough on the generation that died in the wilderness. But flip it around and see it from God's perspective. He brought the Israelites out of a land that had enslaved them for 430 years. He sent a deliverer (Moses) to lead them like a shepherd leading a flock, rolled back the Red Sea so they could cross through on dry ground, made water spring from a rock when they were thirsty, fed them with a sweet bread from heaven that fell like snowflakes, caused their shoes and clothing to never wear out—the list goes on and on.

We see how the people complained against God repeatedly, longed for Egypt, cursed their present circumstances (does any of this sound familiar?), and forgot the God who was practically leading them by the hand. It broke God's heart. It also stirred Him to anger.

Eventually, God had enough and told Moses that the generation that came out of Egypt would never see the Promised Land, but their children would. That means *every single one* of the grumblers and complainers got buried in the wilderness, never seeing the land "flowing with milk and honey."

When Moses died, after seeing the Promised Land on the horizon, God was ready to move forward with the new generation and a new leader. Do you remember the story? As Israel sat camped just outside the borders of Canaan, they sent in twelve spies to spy out the land and bring back a report of what lay ahead. Ten spies brought back a bad report; only two—Joshua and Caleb—brought back a good report.

Listen to the words of Scripture:

The Lord said to Moses, "Send some men to explore the land of Canaan, which I am giving to the Israelites. From each ancestral tribe, send one of its leaders."

When Moses sent them to explore Canaan, he said, "Go up through the Negev and on into the hill country. See what the land is like and whether the people who live there are strong or weak, few or many. What kind of land do they live in? Is it good or bad? What kind of towns do they live in? Are they unwalled or fortified? How is the soil? Is it fertile or poor? Are there trees in it or not? Do your best to bring back some of the fruit of the land." (It was the season for the first ripe grapes.) … At the end of forty days, they returned from exploring the land.

They gave Moses this account: "We went into the land to which you sent us, and it does flow with milk and honey! Here is its fruit. But the people who live there are powerful, and the cities are fortified and very large. We even saw descendants of Anak there. ²⁹ The Amalekites live in the Negev; the Hittites, Jebusites, and Amorites live in the hill country; and the Canaanites live near the sea and along the Jordan."

Then Caleb silenced the people before Moses and said, "We should go up and take possession of the land, for we can certainly do it."

But the men who had gone up with him said, "We can't attack those people; they are stronger than we are." And they spread among the Israelites a bad report about the land they had explored. They said, "The land we explored devours those living in it. All the people we saw there are of great size. We saw the Nephilim there (the descendants of Anakcome from the Nephilim). We seemed like grasshoppers in our own eyes, and we looked the same to them."

Joshua 13:1-2, 17-20, 25, 27-33 NIV (emphasis added)

You can imagine the excitement in the camp of Israel. Here they were, on the borders of the very land they'd been hearing about their whole lives. Remember, their parents had died in the wilderness, so now the *younger* generation is charged with doing what Mom and Dad had failed to do for God. God had brought them through, taken them right up to the borders of Canaan, and said, "Go! I've given this land to you."

Only one little problem: the land is already occupied by other people, some of whom are descendants of giants. God is testing their faith. He's saying, "Have I not shown Myself faithful to deliver you from the Egyptians? Have I not shown Myself faithful to lovingly feed you by My own hand in the wilderness? Am I suddenly going to desert you on the verge of taking this land?" NO! The Lord God of Abraham, Isaac, and Jacob (notice He's not called the God of Terah...hmmm) is faithful to do that which He declares by His Word.

The "bad report" brought back by ten of the spies is actually called an *evil report* in some translations of the Bible. Why does God consider it evil? Because it puts fear into the people and makes them forget about God, forget to rely on His strength, and look at the situation from their own eyes: "We seemed like grasshoppers in our own eyes." Sight is the opposite of faith. It wasn't that they couldn't obtain it; they didn't see the Land (The Promise).

Back to our poppy field analogy, the people were teetering on the brink of behaving just like their parents—the ones God caused to die in the wilderness for their doubt and unbelief, their grumbling and complaining. You could also call it complacency or getting too comfortable.

Not Safe, But Good

C.S. Lewis, an English literature professor and former atheist who became probably the most famous Christian apologist of the twentieth century, wrote the following in his book *The Lion, the Witch, and the Wardrobe*. In the scene, a group of children are talking to Mr. and Mrs. Beaver about meeting a lion named Aslan, who represents Christ in the allegory:

"Is he—quite safe? I shall feel rather nervous about meeting a lion."

"That you will, dearie, and no mistake," said Mrs. Beaver. "If there's anyone who can appear before Aslan without their knees knocking, they're either braver than most or else just silly."

"Then he isn't safe?" said Lucy.

"Safe?" said Mr. Beaver; "don't you hear what Mrs. Beaver tells you? Who said anything about safe? 'Course he isn't safe. But he's good. He's the King, I tell you."

No, our God isn't "safe;" He isn't "gentle Jesus, meek and mild" like the Sunday school song says. The Word declares, "For our God is a consuming fire." Never forget that the God who called you out of darkness and into His marvelous light will always call you to do the brave thing, the bold thing, the crazy thing that may look like it doesn't make sense in the natural world, but "God uses the foolish things of the world to confound the wise."

It's been said, "If your dream doesn't scare you, it isn't big enough." I'll revise that a bit and say, "When God puts a dream or vision in your heart, it will always be something you can't do on your own." He'll make sure you *have* to lean on Him to get it done, look to Him for wisdom, and depend on Him for provision.

Be Strong And Very Courageous

Back to our story with the Israelites. The whole camp is in uproar; ten spies come back and say, "We're crazy to think we can take this land. Let's turn back!" and two say, "Let's roll! God is with us; how can we fail?"

And guess what? The people rebel! Not too surprising, right? Many of us might have done the same thing. They shout,

"Why is the Lord bringing us to this land only to let us fall by the sword? Our wives and children will be taken as plunder. Wouldn't it be better for us to go back to Egypt?" And they said to each other, "We should choose a leader and go back to Egypt" (Numbers 14:3-4 NIV).

Here's how the scene plays out:

Then Moses and Aaron fell face down in front of the whole Israelite assembly gathered there. Joshua, son of Nun, and Caleb, son of Jephunneh, who were among those who had explored the land, tore their clothes and said to the entire Israelite assembly, "The land we passed through and explored is exceedingly good. If the Lord is pleased with us, he will lead us into that land, a land flowing with milk and honey, and will give it to us. Only do not rebel against the Lord . And do not be afraid of the people of the land, because we will devour them. Their protection is gone, but the Lord is with us. Do not be afraid of them."

Numbers 14:5-9 NIV

The angry mob of people wanted to stone them, but then God shows up in all His glory and thunders:

> "...as surely as I live and as surely as the glory of the Lord fills the whole earth, not one of those who saw my glory and the signs I performed in Egypt and in the wilderness but who disobeyed me and tested me ten times—not one of them will ever see the land I promised on oath to their ancestors. No one who has treated me with contempt will ever see it. But because my servant Caleb has a different spirit and follows me wholeheartedly, I will bring him into the land he went to, and his descendants will inherit it."
> Numbers 14:21-24 NIV (emphasis added)

Later, as Joshua, the new leader of Israel, is about to lead the people into Canaan, God delivers a word to him:

> "Moses, my servant, is dead. Now then, you and all these people, get ready to cross the Jordan River into the land I am about to give to them—to the Israelites. I will give you every place where you set your foot, as I promised Moses... No one will be able to stand against you all the days of your life. As I was with Moses, so I will be with you; I will never leave you nor forsake you. Be strong and courageous, because you will lead these people to inherit the land I swore to their ancestors to give them.
>
> "Be strong and very courageous. Be careful to obey all the law my servant Moses gave you; do not turn from it to the right or to the left, that you may be successful wherever you go. Keep this Book of the Law always on your lips; meditate on it day and night, so that you may be careful to do everything written in it. Then you will be prosperous and successful. Have I not commanded you? Be strong and courageous. Do not be afraid; do not be discouraged, for the Lord your God will be with you wherever you go."
>
> So Joshua ordered the officers of the people: "Go through the

camp and tell the people, 'Get your provisions ready. Three days from now you will cross the Jordan here to go in and take possession of the land the Lord your God is giving you for your own.'"

Joshua 1:2-3, 5-11 NIV (emphasis added)

How many times did God say, "Be strong and courageous"? All right, I made it easy for you, but you get the point. Can't you just picture this scene, kind of like William Wallace in *Braveheart* riding back and forth in front of his warriors, preparing them to go into battle. Joshua is talking to the "fighting men" of Israel specifically, and to the whole nation of Israel generally. He's reminding them of everything God has said—and most of all that they are to be strong and very courageous.

Please don't miss this, my brothers and sisters. As we pave our own Yellow Brick Roads with the Word, we too are called to be bold and very courageous. We are called to "press on toward the goal to win the prize for which God has called [us] heavenward in Christ Jesus" (Philippians 3:14 NIV).

Complacency—the poppy field—has no place in our lives. Yes, we all need to take a break from the fray now and then, but don't linger there. Get back to what God has called you to do.

Let me end this chapter with a question: are you, like Caleb, a person of a "different spirit"? Can it be said of you that you too follow the Lord wholeheartedly?

We always have a choice. I hope you choose yes. And every time you come up against something in your path that seems insurmountable, I hope you know where to run for answers. Proverbs 18:10 (NASB) says, "The name of the Lord is a strong tower; the righteous runs into it and is safe." I hope you too can shout, "I See the Land." The promise for your marriage, for your addictions, for your fear, for your insecurities, for your...

Most of all, I hope you have the *boldness to ask...*

11

MEETING OZ
THE BOLDNESS TO ASK

Dorothy starts out her journey singing songs with joy and filling each person she encounters with hope. However, when they finally meet Oz, they are immediately frightened by his theatrics that show a voice of anger and thunder roaring and are too scared to be bold.

Do you ever feel that way when coming to God? From the mouths of men, we hear all these things about how God is harsh and how we should fear Him, and maybe that's what we see played out in Dorothy's encounter with Oz. We soon find out that the Wizard of Oz is only a man behind a microphone.

A lot of us have an unhealthy fear of God because we were told things like "wait till your father gets home" when we were growing up. We always paint a picture that the Father is going to get us whenever we do something wrong, never a picture of One who loves us and gives direction, wisdom, and understanding. In John 14, when Jesus is comforting the Twelve about His impending departure (His death and resurrection), the following conversation ensues:

Thomas said to him, "Lord, we don't know where you are going, so how can we know the way?"

Jesus answered, "I am the way and the truth and the life. No one comes to the Father except through me. If you really know me, you will know my Father as well. From now on, you do know him and have seen him."

Philip said, "Lord, show us the Father, and that will be enough for us."

Jesus answered: "Don't you know me, Philip, even after I have been among you such a long time? Anyone who has seen me has seen the Father."

John 14:5-9 NIV (emphasis added)

How much about God are you willing to believe from the mouths of man? Wouldn't you rather know Him for yourself? I mean, church is important because we need the Body of Christ to come together as God designed it, but if we do not have an accurate, personal understanding of God as our Father, we will never know our place or position as His kids.

Let us, therefore, come boldly to the throne of grace, that we may obtain mercy and find grace to help in time of need.

Hebrews 4:16 NKJV

Therefore, brethren, having boldness to enter the Holiest by the blood of Jesus...

Hebrews 10:19 NKJV

...according to the eternal purpose which He accomplished in Christ Jesus our Lord, in Whom we have boldness and access with confidence through faith in Him.

Ephesians 3: 11-12 NKJV

Saints, because of the blood of Jesus and the spirit of adoption, get to approach God with boldness. I don't think enough of us know this because most of us approach God the way that Dorothy and her crew did. Are you coming to God by chance, knowing that He *can*, but not sure if He *will*? The Bible instructs us to come to God boldly, with joy and confidence. God wants us to be bold while making our requests known to Him.

When we think of boldness, we can't ascribe some weak Christian definition to it. We need to take a good look at what this word means so that we can know exactly how we are supposed to approach God. We also need to know about the blood that grants us free access.

Remember, this is all God's idea. Some people will look at how we approach God and think we are prideful and arrogant. And I'm sure that would be the case if it were our idea, but it was God's idea to begin with.

Everything We Ever Need

When Adam and Eve sinned against God, they handed their—and all of humanity's—authority over to the enemy. He didn't take it without their consent. The enemy can only take what's given to him, and because humanity came into agreement with his lie, he was able to take it from us rightfully.

When Dorothy first meets Oz, he makes a certain request of her: "Get the witch's broom." Dorothy already had the ruby-red slippers (access), but now she needed to get the broom (authority) to take back control of the kingdom. And how does she do it? We see how the Wicked Witch of the West is destroyed by a bucket of water.

The Word of God is also referred to as water, and it is powerful to destroy the wicked and all evil. Dorothy is easily able to strip the witch of her authority with one bucket of water (one Word).

If only we could grasp how powerful the Word of God is in the tearing down of strongholds; in other words, as I said before, the lie that holds you hostage!

.   .   .

When was the last time you were bold in your request to God because of the blood of Jesus that covers you? When was the last time you got in your prayer closet, and because you knew that something was the will of God, you boldly sought Him for counsel and answers? When was the last time you walked up to God, unflinching, unshrinking, and bold?

Dorothy was on a mission to meet the Wizard of Oz, based upon his reputation of doing marvelous works. She was so convinced of his capabilities that she dared to invite the Scarecrow, the Tin Man, and the Lion confidently along with her on her journey. Did you know there is a scriptural precedent for this? *Precedent* is a legal term that sets a standard to be upheld in future cases regarding similar circumstances. What this means is that anyone can point back to the first time something was honored legally, and they can use it as a reference to why the same thing should be honored for them.

> Moreover, concerning a foreigner, who is not of Your people Israel, but has come from a far country for the sake of Your great name and Your mighty hand and Your outstretched arm, when they come and pray in this temple; then hear from heaven Your dwelling place, and do according to all for which the foreigner calls You, that all peoples of the earth may know Your name and fear You, as do Your people Israel, and that they may know that this temple which I have built is called by Your Name.
> 2 Chronicles 6:32-33 NKJV

Considering that Dorothy was a foreigner in Oz, and she based her expectations off his good reputation, how much more should we be able to come with boldness to the throne of God, based on the reputation of Jesus our Lord? How much more confidence should we have when approaching God, knowing that He already paved the way through Jesus?

You see, Dorothy went to Oz hoping that he would help her, based on what other people said about him. We get to go to God based on who He is and based upon what He's already done for us. He already made the way possible, and we should approach Him knowing that He is a good God.

In summary, the Scarecrow thought he needed a brain, the Tin Man was concerned that he didn't have a heart, the Lion thought he needed "nerve" or courage, and Dorothy thought she'd never get back home. We find that, after meeting Oz, each of these characters only needed to be affirmed. The Scarecrow needed to know that he *had* a brain and that his mind was useful. The Lion needed to know that he was courageous already. The Tin Man needed to know that he was loved, and Dorothy needed to know that she could get back home anytime she wanted.

At the end of this story, we see that Oz's balloon starts flying off without Dorothy. As I watched this scene unfold again (while writing this book), I quickly thought how no manmade way can take us to the place we call Home. The Good Holy Spirit shows up—I mean the Good Witch shows up—and reminds Dorothy that all she has to do is tap her red shoes three times—tap one, the Father; tap two, the Son; and tap three, the Holy Spirit—and she will get back home.

God created us with everything we would ever need.

See, in *The Wizard of Oz*, Dorothy longed to go to a place that was "over the rainbow." In other words, a place where all her troubles would go away. I believe the rainbow represents the promises of God, so on the other side would be heavenly results. She was certain that this trouble-free place would be her home. But along her journey toward that home, Dorothy encountered a whole lot of trouble, evil witches, scary forests with monkeys, moments where she would have to confront her fears. What she didn't realize at the time was that she needed to go through Oz to get to a better understanding of who she really was. The troubles in Oz were her storms on the road to understanding her true identity—a better appreciation of her own home and family in Kansas.

Storms give us the opportunity to encounter God, to mature, and to be prepared for the bigger things yet to come.

Wisdom Calls From The Crossroads

One day as I was reading through Proverbs, a verse jumped out at me. Everything God had been speaking to me about Dorothy on the Yellow Brick Road, and immediately coming to a *crossroads*, made my heart leap in my chest. Listen to the words of Proverbs 8:1-17:

Listen as Wisdom calls out!
    Hear as understanding raises her voice!
On the hilltop along the road,
    she takes her stand at the crossroads.
By the gates at the entrance to the town,
    on the road leading in, she cries aloud,
"I call to you, to all of you!
    I raise my voice to all people.
You simple people, use good judgment.
    You foolish people, show some understanding.
Listen to me! For I have important things to tell you.
    Everything I say is right,
for I speak the truth
    and detest every kind of deception.
My advice is wholesome.
    There is nothing devious or crooked in it.
My words are plain to anyone with understanding,
    clear to those with knowledge.
Choose my instruction rather than silver,
    and knowledge rather than pure gold.
For wisdom is far more valuable than rubies.
    Nothing you desire can compare with it.
"I, Wisdom, live together with good judgment.
    I know where to discover knowledge and discernment.
All who fear the Lord will hate evil.
    Therefore, I hate pride and arrogance,
    corruption and perverse speech.
Common sense and success belong to me.

Insight and strength are mine.
Because of me, kings reign,
    and rulers make just decrees.
Rulers lead with my help,
    and nobles make righteous judgments.
"I love all who love me.
    Those who search will surely find me."

I want to end this book the same way I started it. If you're in a mess, it's because you're complicating God's promise with your way of doing things. Right now, you're stuck and things aren't working. James Allen says people are anxious to improve their circumstances, but are unwilling to improve themselves; therefore, they remain bound. The Bible says as a man thinketh, so is he. Maybe it's time to surrender your ways for his ways.

You've come to a crossroads.

I don't know your story. I don't know what issues you're facing. But I do know something undeniable: we serve a big God, and there is only one way, one road, to that place called "over the rainbow."

My prayer is that you will pave every step you take on this earth— the path God has called you to walk—with heaven's streets of gold.

Your very own Yellow Brick Road.

INVITATION

Do you want to get wrapped with Jesus? Here's where you begin your own walk along streets of gold.

Getting Saved

If you want to get right with God, here is a sample prayer. Remember, saying this prayer or any other prayer will not save you, and neither will raising your hand or going down the aisle to an altar. Surrendering your heart to Jesus Christ is the only way. But let's start somewhere like reading this prayer:

"God, I know that I have sinned against You and am deserving of your wrath. But your son, Jesus Christ, died on the cross and took the punishment that I deserve, so that through faith in Him, I could be forgiven. I place my trust in You for salvation. Thank You for Your grace and forgiveness—and the gift of eternal life! In Jesus's name, Amen!"

He asked for your hand in marriage, and you said YES! Congratulations.

Remember earlier in the book I told you it takes a lifetime to manufacture a saint? Okay, so now the work begins, but it will be worth it. Jesus is the groom, and everything about Christianity is about becoming one with your spouse. He goes with me everywhere I go, but everywhere I go, I go with Him in my heart.

Begin your journey by getting connected with a body of believers (church) and allow him to order your steps by way of His Word. Meditate on them day and night, and you will be blessed in all that you do. These are beautiful verses to get you started:

- "For God so loved the world that he gave his one and only Son, that whoever believes in him shall not perish but have eternal life" (John 3:16).

- "Believe in the Lord Jesus, and you will be saved" (Acts 16:31).

- God has already done all of the work. All you must do is receive, in faith, the salvation God offers (Ephesians 2:8-9).

ACKNOWLEDGMENTS

I want to start by thanking my beautiful wife, Ruthy. My baby RUTH, you have always believed in me and stood with me through all the stressful and crazy days. Thank you for loving me the way you do and for always reminding me that I was made for greatness.

I want to thank Phillip Baker who played a major role with one word—GO;

Vinny and Sara for always believing in me and the vision God has given us to build the Kingdom; Gregg and Michelle for always pushing me to do great things; my assistant Stephanie you are one of a kind thank you for all the honor and how you left everything to serve Ruthy and I.

Amber you have been with us for years and when it all started, thank you for assisting in the beginning of this project. Jack and Nora for all your support you guys have been angels; Rosita our first partner thank you, and the whole Get Wrapped family for all your LOVE and encouraging words along the way.

Robert and Richard Olivo, actually the whole Olivo family, for always pushing me to do the impossible and taking me into your family as a little brother.

Gateway Church—Wow, wow, wow is all I can say. Thank you for the wise counsel. Pastor David Vestal, you're a champ who would of thought God would give me a narcotics detective as a mentor (LOL). Bishop Tony Miller thank you for the Gatherings and the Timothy Team. You're one of a kind and full of wisdom.

To Dr. Scott Silverii and the team at Five Stones Press; thank you for walking with me along this book journey. I could not have finished without you.

John Ramirez, as you would say, Brothaaaaaaaaa, lol. Thank you for sticking with me like white on rice, and I appreciate you and love you for staying on me about writing a book or books.

All Nations School of Ministry for helping me walk this out in the beginning. John Maxwell team, thank you for teaching me about leadership.

All my kiddos, Jay, Nina, Jonathan, Valery, Johnathan and Josh, for being so awesome and for cheering for me as I wrote it.

I want to honor my spiritual parents Billy and Vinnie Yarborough you guys have been Jesus walking the earth. Mrs. Vinnie you always believed in me and spoke things to me that brought me comfort and thrusted me forward.

Pastor Dennis Hall, with New Life Church, for being such a big part of the impact we were able to have in Breckenridge. Way back in the beginning, they were some of the first people that came alongside me, even when they didn't know me.

Finally, my mom, Elsa, for always praying and never giving up on the promises of God for me, for paving the streets that I walk on today, you are my hero.

ABOUT THE AUTHOR

Juan Martinez is the founder of Wrapped in the Love of Christ Ministry and serves as the senior pastor of the Get Wrapped Church in Spring, Texas. Since 2010, the ministry has seen thousands of people say yes to Christ. Juan's heart and main focus is simply winning souls by wrapping them in the *love of Christ*.

Through dynamic ministering of the Word of God, Juan is a true revivalist with a burning *passion* and a deep desire to see the lost saved, the broken mended, the afflicted healed, and the body of Christ operate in its God-given authority.

God has transformed him from having a killing, stealing, and destroying mentality to a seed-sowing mindset, spreading the Good

News to all who will listen. He has seen God move miraculously in his life and has a hunger for all of creation to experience the same.

Additionally, Juan is involved in speaking at various conferences, partnering in outreaches (all around the United States), and is the coauthor of the international bestseller *Share Your Message with the World*. Juan and his wife, Ruthy, have six children: Janina, Valery, Jonathan, Jay, Johnathan, and Joshua.

From left to right Jonathan, Josh, Valery, Me, Baby Ruth, Johnathan, Jay and Janina

---

This Is Real Radio - www.juanmartinez.tv
Podcast - https://podcasts.subsplash.com/m3bb5k3/podcast.rss
Get Wrapped Church - www.getwrapped.tv

facebook.com/juanmartinez.tv
instagram.com/lovewinsu
youtube.com/ThisIsRealWithJuanMartinez